A Guide to Faculty-Led Study Abroad

A Guide to Faculty-Led Study Abroad provides practical information on the curricular and administrative considerations necessary to design and implement a course-based study abroad experience of the highest quality. From techniques for funding the trip, to legal considerations, curricular development, and cultural preparation, this book explains how to create a meaningful and valuable international experience in a variety of settings and formats. The study abroad novice and experienced faculty or administrator alike will benefit from this step-by-step guide on how to create a truly transformative, course-based study abroad experience.

Lydia M. Andrade is a Professor of Government and International Affairs at the University of the Incarnate Word, USA.

Scott Dittloff is a Professor of Government and International Affairs at the University of the Incarnate Word, USA.

Lopita Nath is Professor and Chair of the Department of History at the University of the Incarnate Word, USA.

A Guide to Faculty-Led Study Abroad

How to Create a Transformative Experience

Lydia M. Andrade,
Scott Dittloff, and
Lopita Nath

NEW YORK AND LONDON

First published 2019
by Routledge
52 Vanderbilt Avenue, New York, NY 10017

and by Routledge
2 Park Square, Milton Park, Abingdon, Oxon, OX14 4RN

Routledge is an imprint of the Taylor & Francis Group, an informa business

© 2019 Taylor & Francis

The right of Lydia M. Andrade, Scott Dittloff, and Lopita Nath to be identified as authors of this work has been asserted by them in accordance with sections 77 and 78 of the Copyright, Designs and Patents Act 1988.

All rights reserved. No part of this book may be reprinted or reproduced or utilised in any form or by any electronic, mechanical, or other means, now known or hereafter invented, including photocopying and recording, or in any information storage or retrieval system, without permission in writing from the publishers.

Trademark notice: Product or corporate names may be trademarks or registered trademarks, and are used only for identification and explanation without intent to infringe.

Library of Congress Cataloging-in-Publication Data
A catalog record for this title has been requested

ISBN: 978-0-8153-7693-4 (hbk)
ISBN: 978-0-8153-7696-5 (pbk)
ISBN: 978-1-351-23506-8 (ebk)

Typeset in Perpetua
by codeMantra

Contents

Preface		vii
Acknowledgments		xiii
1	Teaching Study Abroad	1
2	Before You Say Yes	13
3	Planning the Trip	21
4	What to Teach	56
5	The Budget	73
6	Responsibility	97
7	So, Are You Ready?	114
8	On Ground	121
9	How Far Is Too Far?	146
10	Is It Worth It?	157
	Additional Resources	161
	Index	167

Preface

WHY STUDY ABROAD?

Our first trip was to London in 2005. It was memorable for many reasons. First of all, there were 35 of us, with approximately two-thirds of the group being high school girls. Among other things, this meant that we had to schedule the entire day for all 11 days we were in London and environs (we made day trips to Windsor Castle and Oxford). The parents of the high school girls who were traveling with us did not want them to have any unsupervised time. If that were not enough, we decided to plan the entire trip ourselves, from airline to lodging to transportation between sites during the day. We did this to keep the costs down and because another faculty member who was coming with us said he knew London well. We counted on him to provide the on-ground understanding and experience to help us calculate sufficient time for all of the activities, to determine how long it would take to get where we were going, and to know the city well enough to help find appropriate restaurants, etc.

As it turned out, our "London expert" didn't provide much assistance in planning the schedule, and as we got closer to the departure date, he became thoroughly disengaged, and a couple of inexperienced faculty had to take over. We learned a very valuable lesson though; if you are leading the trip, YOU are responsible for everything! Get to know your destination thoroughly before leaving the country. We knew the landscape of London almost better than our own city by the time we arrived. We read and re-read web-sites, tourist guides, maps, and reviews from both colleagues and unknown tourists so many times that we knew almost down to the minute how long it would take to get from any destination on our itinerary to the next destination. We also figured out how to maximize our travel time from destination to destination by plotting out each day ahead of time. When unexpected events caused us to make changes, we could easily readjust our itinerary without wasting time crisscrossing the city on The Tube.

PREFACE

> Even the best research may fail you from time to time. Based on recommendations from travel guides and on-line reviews, we had scheduled an hour and a half at the Cabinet War Rooms (CWR) in the Imperial War Museum (IWM). However, our students found the CWR so interesting that we spent over three hours there. We decided on the fly to let them stay longer at the CWR, scrubbed the next destination (about a 10-minute walk across the Thames), and walked the short distance to our final destination of the day (for which we had a reserved entrance time). The nice thing about planning the trip ourselves and tailoring it for our class was that, just as is the case in our classrooms, we were free to change the plans when student interested demanded more time for certain material.

When we started planning that first trip, we did not foresee the degree of importance that such preparation would have for the students to truly understand the country and places we were going to visit. Luckily, we spent an entire semester providing our students a thorough historical, social, political, cultural, and practical context for our trip. This proved invaluable as the students not only approached the sites we visited with a sense of appreciation for what they were seeing but also were prepared to engage with them. Moreover, they showed the proper respect for St. Paul's Cathedral, Westminster Abbey, Buckingham Palace, and the surprisingly poor performance of *The Tempest* at the Globe Theatre (even our dean, a theater professor, who accompanied us, found the performance so lifeless that she agreed with us leaving at the intermission). As study-abroad newbies, we thought the more the students knew, the better. It was only several years (and trips) later that we learned how right we were about preparation and the consequences of the lack thereof.

As a result of our experiences on that first trip, we now require those traveling with us to participate in significant pre-departure academic preparation. Despite this, we have had, on a few occasions, students from other universities who had not been in our preparatory courses. This has usually meant that we have had no idea about their level of preparation or academic exposure, and this has often led to these students' not taking the travel part of the class very seriously, not necessarily behaving as we would hope, and not learning quite as much as our students. The success experienced with students who follow our model of preparation (and lack thereof in other cases) has convinced us that we have developed a powerful study abroad pedagogy. The literature on study abroad, which we will cover in the next section, overwhelmingly supports our approach.

PREFACE

> In an attempt to be creative, find additional resources, and work with a sister institution, we once planned a trip to India, combining our trip with that of another group of students from another university. Their faculty member taught the students at the other university more or less the same material we taught, and we scheduled several video conferences during the semester, so the students would get to meet each other and begin to build a little esprit de corps before traveling. While we tried to make the two groups have comparable pre-departure experiences and expectations, we soon found out that this was not the case.
>
> A last-minute emergency prevented the other faculty member from traveling, so a staff person was assigned as a chaperone. Additionally, the students from the other university traveled on their own to India (which we do not permit), with a couple of students arriving the day before we did. Upon learning of this, we scrambled to provide an itinerary for those students for the day before any faculty or staff from either school arrived. However, on that first night (before our arrival), the students consumed over $1,000.00 of alcohol from the mini-bar in their room. Being hungover the next morning, they simply did not show up for the activities planned (and paid for) specifically for them. And that was just the beginning. The other group was problematic throughout the trip as they did not respect their chaperone and acted as if their vacation was being rudely interrupted by our academic expectations. In short, the antithesis of our educational goals.

We have traveled overseas with a pregnant student, a student who had a hole in their heart, students who have bi-polar disorder, students with anxiety issues, students with post-traumatic stress disorder (PTSD), and one who ended up in the hospital for almost a week during the trip after having a psychotic episode. We have made trips to various medical clinics around the world for strep throat (that got passed around among most of the travelers), rashes, and lost inhalers. But we have also seen the Great Wall, the Taj Mahal, the Berlin Wall, and the Louvre, ridden an elephant (multiple times), traveled in an auto rickshaw, had an impromptu wine tasting in Germany, saw the American sector of the D-Day invasion, sang *The Sound of Music* songs while running in the garden in Salzburg, and tasted (and liked!) a banana latte and a sweet potato latte in South Korea.

While we spend an enormous amount of time preparing not only the trip but the students ahead of time, we spend just as much time while abroad engaging with our students. We constantly emphasize the academic component of the trip and look for teachable moments to keep the students engaged and modeling the appropriate behavior both before and during the trip. And while we do not

PREFACE

program them or chaperone them 24 hours a day, we do consider ourselves to be on call during the entire trip. We are not only the leaders of the trip—we are an integral part of the learning experience and sometimes a much-needed parent.

All in all, we have taken over 150 students to 10 different countries in a little over 12 years. We have also taken students to Washington, D.C.; New York; and Boston multiple times, bringing the number of students we have led to over 200.

At this point, you may be asking yourself why we would do this. The answer is straightforward: It is good for the students, it is good for the university, and it is good for us. Understanding the world around us has always been a central component of a liberal education. A liberal education is associated with the development of the student as a whole person who values life-long learning. We are helping to cultivate active citizens who help to support and protect society while at the same time giving them the tools to adapt as society and the world change (so they remain socially, politically, and economically relevant). With globalization, the world is changing at an increasingly rapid rate, forcing us all to become global citizens. Global citizenship requires the ability to understand and work with people from different cultures. These "intercultural competencies" are the skills necessary for promoting successful collaboration across cultures (Hammer, Bennett, and Wiseman 2003 and Bennett, Bennett, and Allen 2003). Study abroad is an ideal means for not only introducing intercultural competencies and understandings but also practicing them.

Despite its importance and the increasing emphasis that higher education has put on study abroad, internationalizing the curriculum, and intercultural competencies, only 1.6% of U.S. students study abroad (NAFSA 2018). So, if the students won't go to the world, we have to bring the world to them. An important element of study abroad which sometimes is overlooked is the value of student travelers bringing back to campus their new knowledge and insights. Many of our students are transformed by their international experiences. They continue to travel on their own, with some taking jobs overseas and all of them seeing issues through a more global lens. They come back as ambassadors of international travel and study, and help infuse the campus with an international flavor, bringing a passion for new cultures, styles, music, food, and languages. Through formal presentations, university-sponsored campus cultural events (e.g., Asian New Year Celebration), and word of mouth, those who have studied abroad bring the world back to the campus community.

For the faculty, leading a course-based study abroad experience can be personally and professionally enriching. Travel may provide a sense of communion with the world or just provide an opportunity to expand your own horizons. Your teaching at home can also be substantially enhanced by your international experiences. If your teaching and research areas are international, study abroad will give you more examples to draw from, opportunities to deepen your knowledge, and new-found enthusiasm for your topic.

PREFACE

Even if your teaching and research fields are not distinctly international in perspective (or if you come from a field in which such comparisons are irrelevant), you learn about differences that may bring context to your material. For example, simply talking about or teaching the importance of portion size in a nutrition class is one thing, but having spent time in Europe, where the portions are smaller and everyone walks everywhere, gives faculty credibility in explaining this to students.

We believe that we have developed a successful model for course-based study abroad. It is hard work, but when done well, it is rewarding for us personally, for our students, and for our campus. In this book, we describe the model for you and take you step by step through the process. Whether you are taking students abroad for the first time or the 10th time, or are merely considering it, we are here to help answer your questions and prepare you for what will surely be an adventure.

WHY WE WROTE THIS BOOK AND HOW IT IS STRUCTURED

Given the number of times we have done this, we are regularly asked for advice by faculty and administrators, and thus we have written this book as a "how to do course-based study abroad" manual. Each chapter covers one aspect of preparing for or teaching a course-based study abroad course. We have tried to be thorough, but given the variety of courses, institutions, and destinations possible, we apologize in advance if we have forgotten anything. Nevertheless, we think you will find that our approach and discussions will provide guidance, even if we do not address the exact nature of your course.

The structure for each chapter will follow a similar pattern: We explain our ideas and recommendations on a different topic area following the process of planning, teaching, and implementing a course-based study abroad trip. Real-life examples experienced by the authors, our co-workers, and our friends will be used to highlight our suggestions. At the conclusion of every chapter, there will be a checkoff list that you can use to guide the development of your own course-based study abroad trip. There is also an extensive bibliography to allow you to examine almost any study abroad topic in more detail.

We begin by providing an overview of the literature on study abroad and the importance of globalizing the curriculum. Then we move on to the specific discussion of "how to" in Chapter Two, entitled "Before You Say Yes," with an overview of what to expect of traveling with students, what questions to ask yourself, and what questions to ask your institution before deciding whether to take students abroad. Chapter Three, "Planning the Trip," guides you through the various administrative and practical steps in the preparation of a course-based study abroad class. The need to tie travel destinations and experiences to specific curricular

PREFACE

activities is explained, and a timeline is provided for completing all that is necessary for a successful trip. Chapter Four explores the idea of "What to Teach" to prepare students for travel and how to integrate the travel into the curriculum. The budgeting chapter details the creation of budgets for the program, focusing on how to determine the total cost, being prepared for unexpected costs, and how to prepare for the students' as well as your own costs. Chapter Six explores the legal and professional responsibilities of faculty leading student travel. We discuss conversations that faculty should have with their administration prior to travel concerning student selection, liability, and institutional support before and during the study abroad experience as well as what could go wrong and how to deal with that. Chapter Seven explains the pre-departure research that faculty should do to ensure that once on ground, all goes smoothly. Chapter Eight, entitled "On Ground," is where we present the experience as it will play out while traveling as well as information on dealing with the students when on the trip. We offer recommendations about how to manage the students and the itinerary to get the most out of your time in-country. In Chapter Nine, "How Far Is Too Far?," we discuss the challenges that even the most modest international experience may pose for students and discuss ways to prevent and accommodate for these issues. Finally, in Chapter Ten, we ask "Is It Worth It?" Here, we offer some concluding remarks about the value of the study abroad experience—for the student, instructor, department, and institution—and whether all the work is worth it.

So, go ahead, and go! Have a nice trip! Bon voyage! Goede reis! Magandang biyahe! Gute reise! Turas maith! Buon viaggio! Tutum! haerenga pai! God tur! Dobra podróż! Boa viagem! Buen viaje! Safari nzuri! Bra resa! Iyi yolculuk! Daith da! Uhambo oluhle! Irin-ajo to dara! Uhambo oluhle!

REFERENCES

Bennett, Janet M., Milton J. Bennett and Wendy Allen. 2003. "Developing Intercultural Competence in the Language Classroom." In D.L. Lange & R.M. Paige, eds. *Culture at the Core: Perspectives on Culture in Second Language Learning*. Greenwich, CN: Information Age Publishing.

Hammer, Mister R., Bennett, Milton J. and Wiseman, R. 2003. "Measuring intercultural competence: The Intercultural Development Inventory." In guest ed. R. M. Paige, Special Issue on Intercultural Development. *International Journal of Intercultural Relations* 27 (4): 421–443.

NAFSA. 2018. "Trends in U.S. Study Abroad." www.nafsa.org/Policy_and_Advocacy/Policy_Resources/Policy_Trends_and_Data/Trends_in_U_S__Study_Abroad/ (Accessed June 26, 2018).

Acknowledgments

There are a host of people who have taught us about study abroad, whether consciously or not. There are, however, a number of people who we would like to recognize for their contributions to our travels and learning experiences over the years.

To our travel agent Gail, who booked innumerable trips, guided our choices, rescued us from potential disasters, and over the years became a dear friend, thank you! You are the best!

To our international partners who have helped plan and traveled with us, thank you:

- Anup Nair & Incentives Destinations: You have been the perfect travel group. You know the destinations so well and have offered suggestions that met our travel objectives, and you took us well beyond our loftiest aspirations. Thank you!
- Tombi Singh: You have been the most kind, generous, gracious, and tolerant tour host one could ask for. The phrase "above and beyond" has become almost a cliché, but you, Tombi, exemplify that in your job and persona. We have loved all our travels with you. The students continue to sing your praises, so thank you!

To Alejandra Yañez Vega, our dear friend and institutional partner. Your collaboration, advice, and always present smile have given us opportunities and experiences we will never forget. Thank you, friend!

To all our friends, colleagues, and administrators at the University of the Incarnate Word (UIW), and particularly a very supportive Dean Vichcales, who have made these opportunities possible, thank you. We could not have done any of this without you.

ACKNOWLEDGMENTS

To our families, who have supported us throughout the many years and trips (and much silliness) and welcomed us home, even though they never get to go with us—we love you!

And finally, to our students, who have taught us many valuable lessons—you have made us laugh; cry; and, yes, even yell sometimes, but most importantly, you have shown us the world. We cannot thank you enough. We will never forget you!

Chapter One

Teaching Study Abroad

STUDY ABROAD: THE TRADITIONAL IDEAL

If you are reading this book, you are probably at least thinking about providing your students the opportunity to explore the world and gain the many benefits associated with study abroad. The literature on study abroad details a plethora of benefits from an international experience. Intercultural competence (Root and Ngampornchai 2012), increased levels of international political concern, cross-cultural interest (see Van Gyn, Schuerholz-Lehr, Caws, and Preece 2009; Goodman and Berdan 2014), and cultural cosmopolitanism (Carlson and Widaman 1988; Thomlison 1991; Hadis 2005) may be some of the most obvious benefits of study abroad. The cross-cultural understanding and development of the knowledge, skills, and values needed to successfully engage with those from around the world (Brodin 2010) lead to more engaged global citizenship (Hanson 2010). Gaining new perspectives and a willingness to learn, which often comes with those new perspectives, leads to finding jobs sooner and at higher salaries (Lim, Ho, Wee, and Chu 2016) in one's chosen field (Cook-Anderson 2012). Success in finding a job may be because students who have studied abroad are better at creative thinking (Lee, Therriault, and Linderholm 2012); have developed complex problem-solving skills (Berdan, Goodman, and Taylor 2013); are more independent and open-minded; and have better time management, better organization, better social skills, and greater self-confidence (Hadis 2005; Studyabroad.com 2017). There are indeed many well-established benefits of studying abroad.

Study abroad programs have traditionally involved students studying in another country for an extended period of time, such as a semester or a year. Long-term immersion while learning a foreign language or taking courses in another language combined language learning/acquisition and cultural, social, political, historical, etc. understanding through study of language. Students need to continually speak the language to conduct all aspects of their daily lives. They thus absorb the totality of that country as they *live* the language; they cannot just stop learning/speaking/studying when the class is over.

Study abroad is supposed to open the mind; challenge pre-conceived notions of the world; and expose students to new ideas, peoples, and cultures, expanding the vista of students globally, intellectually, and personally. Douglas and Jones-Rikkers term this development as "worldmindedness," meaning "the extent to which individuals value global perspectives on various issues" (2001). While the developing of worldmindedness sounds like a wonderful goal, it does not always occur in the smooth, good-natured way we might hope. Recent critics of study abroad provide anecdotal reports that find students who study abroad often struggle academically, face social isolation, and have difficulty adjusting to a new culture (Wu, Garza, and Guzman 2015). They may find it difficult to make new friends because of language and cultural challenges, and will often resort to making friends primarily with other study abroad students from their home country because it is easier to converse and because of the general cultural comfort associated with a compatriot. Rather than becoming a positive and enriching experience, the traditional model of study abroad, where an individual goes abroad on her own, can actually undermine the purpose of study abroad, all the while entailing significant cost and inhibiting the development of worldmindedness. For some students, at least, a good study abroad experience needs to provide structure and guidance as well as support, so students do not become isolated and disenchanted, thus jeopardizing the benefits of an international experience. As Tarrant, Rubin, and Stoner (2014) point out, it is not "study abroad alone that nurtures a global citizenry, but that it does have the potential to do so when the academic content and pedagogical delivery is offered in a synergistic fashion."

And while the need for a greater connection between content delivery and travel has been agreed upon by most, the additional concern with the accessibility of study abroad also demands attention. Researchers have begun to decry and demonstrate the inequalities in study abroad. They assert that traditional study abroad programs are often too expensive (Twombly, Salisbury, Tumanut, and Klute 2012, ix) or require too much time away from family or work obligations for many of today's students (Spencer and Tuma 2002). We have definitely seen these to be huge hurdles for our students.

> Over the years, we have had trips that were relatively inexpensive, such as a week trip to the Netherlands (where a sister institution paid for our housing) that only cost about $3,000.00 That included airfare, all on-ground transportation, entrance to all sites, local guides, and meals. We have also had trips become as expensive as $6,200.00 for a month in India. The key aspect in the cost is the lack of funding to cover faculty participation costs. If faculty airfare, hotel, etc. are not funded by the institution, the costs are passed along to the students, increasing the price significantly. These costs can represent a significant hurdle for many students.

Other obstacles which affect participation in study abroad include lack of information, an increasing trend among current students for more limited involvement in co-curricular activities, and attitudes toward and lack of interest in study abroad and the world at large (Twombly, Salisbury, Tumanut, and Klute 2012). We have found that our primarily first-generation college students have rarely considered the possibility of study abroad and have to have the importance of being involved on campus and in extra-curricular activities explained to them. They simply lack exposure to these ideas. Male students, minority students, and those majoring in a non-liberal arts or social science fields are also significantly less likely to participate in traditional study abroad (Twombly, Salisbury, Tumanut, and Klute 2012).

If we truly value study abroad, the question becomes how do we expand participation in study abroad and its benefits? If study abroad is to be encouraged, it must be more accessible. Beginning around 2000, the study abroad research focus turned to the consideration of short-term study abroad (Spencer and Tuma 2002). Short-term study abroad experiences are considered to be those in which students travel for fewer than eight weeks (Donnelly-Smith 2009; Allen 2010). While in 1996–1997, only 3.3 percent of study abroad students participated in short-term programs, by 2008–2009, these programs accounted for 55.4 percent of undergraduate study abroad experiences (see Bhandari and Chow 2008; Donnelly-Smith 2009). Short-term programs have increased in popularity, and yet "...formal research describing the best practices for short-term study abroad or the learning outcomes that can accompany it" (Donnelly-Smith 2009) are in the nascent stage.

THE ARGUMENT FOR COURSE-BASED STUDY ABROAD

Although not fully developed yet, the research on short-term study abroad does indicate that "short-term programs can have a positive impact on the overall development of cross-cultural sensitivity" (Anderson, Lawton, Rexeisen, and Hubbard 2005). Spencer and Tuma (2002) contend that short-term study abroad programs can compensate for the short duration by making the travel a continuation of a process started in the classroom before departure.

> The learning abroad is enhanced in these short-term programs if the experience is preceded by preparatory study. The preparatory study needs to include the logistics of travel, but far more importantly, it must include the academic content that gives focus to the course. Such study allows the students to "hit the ground running," to have an intellectual context into which to fit what they learn abroad.

Our observations support these findings as to the value of solid preparatory study prior to short-term study abroad. Our trips will always have one or more students experiencing a moment where they nod their head and can almost guess what a guide or the faculty is going to say before they say it. It shows that they are attuned to the new experiences and have a foundation upon which to build.

While shorter-term, course-based study abroad is not a solution to the limitations of extended study abroad, such as struggling academically, social isolation, and difficulty adjusting to a new culture, it can be, if properly designed, an integral part of the learning experience for the students and a means to develop intercultural understanding (McKeown 2009). The key is to integrate the travel component of the course with the curriculum (see Tarrant 2010).

INTEGRATING TRAVEL AND CURRICULUM

While integrating the travel with the curriculum may seem almost absurdly obvious, it is not necessarily always accomplished or even consciously attempted. Some may assume that students will automatically "get" the connection of the course material with the travel or that simply visiting places discussed in a class back at the home campus will make them more compelling. This, from our experience, does not simply occur without an overt effort on the part of the faculty to integrate the travel with the curriculum.

So, what do we mean by integrating the travel with the course curriculum? It means that the travel is part of the curriculum, and not just tourism: that there is a curricular purpose to what occurs during a course-based study abroad trip. When planning the travel, faculty must make sure that the sites to be visited and the activities that occur in and around the travel have specific learning objectives that tie into and continue the learning objectives of the course on campus prior to departure. While we generally think of study abroad as experiential learning, meaning that learning occurs through exposure to the sights, sounds, smells, etc. of being in an unfamiliar place, this presumes that study abroad is basically its own discipline. The learning objectives in this case would be cultural, religious, intercultural, and tolerance development. These are the foundational principles of a liberal education. Integration occurs when study abroad learning outcomes are developed, and the travel "curriculum" is planned so that the travel and the academic discipline course objectives are symbiotic. The pedagogical approaches differ, but the learning objectives purposely converge. This travel and traditional academic disciplinary convergence bridges the gap between academic learning and experiential and intercultural learning. The result is a deeper and richer understanding: not just what but why and how.

The travel must be part of the pedagogy of the course, or it is little more than "intellectual tourism" (Hanson 2010). Our goal is to go beyond simply transmitting information or knowledge to create an enhanced learning experience where students learn about course material and hopefully facilitate the development of well-rounded, liberally educated people. Our objective is to cultivate acceptance and understanding of different cultures, religions, and peoples; build intercultural understanding and tolerance; and ultimately foster enlightened global citizens. Our travel starts with that as the foundation, and everything builds from there: where we go, what we see, what we do, how long we travel, and especially how we teach the preparatory course and interact with the students and the material while traveling.

Why Course-Based Study Abroad?

Faculty led, curriculum based, course-based study abroad can help ensure that students are prepared and open to learning about and experiencing the international community. We recommend what some refer to as embedded programs. "Embedded Program (or Course-Embedded [Based] Study Abroad) – [is] a short study abroad experience that forms an integral part of, or an optional add-on to, a course given on the home campus" (Forum on Education Abroad 2011, 14).

As the research on traditional study abroad demonstrates, even the longest periods of immersion do not necessarily guarantee the development of cultural understanding and tolerance. Short-term travel can have even less chance of accomplishing these goals. If they are not prepared with the appropriate historical, cultural, and academic discipline background to understand and process their international experiences, students will not get the most out of their international experience. Our approach, developed over years of traveling with students, is designed to make sure that course curriculum/activities and the travel logistics create a framework which helps students facilitate exploring ideas, cultures, and concepts, and provides the necessary support, so they can focus on learning in a new and sometimes challenging environment.

We are strong supporters of course-based study abroad and the opportunities it provides students. While traditional semester or year-long study abroad is an excellent choice for many students and offers experiences that shorter study abroad trips cannot, we concern ourselves with course-based study abroad for several reasons. It is more affordable than a semester long or full year study abroad. For some students, cost may be of little concern, but for many students, particularly at an institution like ours (a Hispanic Serving Institution [HSI], with a large percentage of first-generation students), a semester or a year abroad is simply out of the question. Moreover, while there are funding opportunities for travel (which we discuss later), many, if not most, of our students work to help pay for their education, and studying abroad for a semester or year would require that they forfeit that support. Not only would they have to raise the funds to pay for the study abroad, but they would also lose the income from their job and likely have to find a new job when they returned. Additionally, students with family obligations may not be able to be gone as long as a semester, and student athletes who rely on scholarships to pay for school that require their participating in sports also may not be able to take a semester off. Time and money are the issues. Thus, for many students, course-based study abroad offers a more accessible experience. Given the increasing importance of negotiating a global economic, social, and political culture, the lack of opportunity to experience other countries, cultures, languages, etc. creates another gap between the haves and the have nots. The affordability and accessibility of course-based study abroad opportunities help to bridge that gap.

Another benefit of course-based study abroad is that it often fits more easily into student degree plans than semester or year-long experiences. On our campus, this is particularly true for those students majoring in degrees such as pre-med or engineering, which may require lab courses that can be a challenge to find away from the home campus. Course-based study abroad classes are part of the curriculum of the university or college the student is attending; therefore, there are no issues with finding specific courses or transferring credits, as there might be with studying abroad at another institution.

Additionally, course-based study abroad engages the students with the country and the topic while still providing a small comfort zone/familiarity with their fellow travelers. For those students who may be hesitant to travel or experience new cultures, this can be a perfect solution. Faculty provide the opportunities for students to engage with the people and culture of a new country (so they can't just isolate themselves), and there is still a group of classmates to provide a bit of grounding or buffering. Any type of international experience has the possibility of enhancing global/international understanding, but if students hesitate to engage, have difficulties adapting, or just become homesick, isolating themselves limits the effects that may accrue from international travel. With faculty closely involved in and actively planning and running the study abroad curriculum, they can create comfortable engagement opportunities; be there to help students understand and process; and, if necessary, just listen, so students realize that they are not alone.

Despite only traveling for a short period, the travel, interacting with others, and having everyday experiences in an unknown/new language or culture teaches students to be flexible and adaptive, and become problem solvers. We saw just how true this was when we took students to India on a service learning trip, and the plan was to have our students teach health and sanitation to the local schoolchildren. The schools, however, closed early that year because of a heat wave. That meant that the school we were going to be working with had no electricity or water. Teaching even simple sanitation lessons, such as the importance of handwashing, without water is difficult; teaching it without students is even more difficult. But we put the word out to the local community that we would offer a summer camp at the school. Our students brainstormed a teaching solution as a group. They modeled the process at the dry faucets and drew faucets on the walls (which the school used as chalkboards), and demonstrated the handwashing procedure. Quick and creative thinking allowed the students to succeed in teaching their lessons, despite not having the essential tools necessary. The adaptation (and the good humor which accompanied it) helped our students gain confidence in their own interpersonal skills, strengthened the group dynamic, and enhanced the students' tolerance and understanding of the challenges faced by others. These skills are incredibly important and will serve them well in the workforce.

Emphasis on Course

Internationalization seems to be the "in" focus for higher education, and as educators, we want to prepare our students to compete in the global marketplace. Perhaps more importantly, we also want our students to be good global citizens. We want them to understand what it means to be a participant in the global community, to recognize that they are part of a larger identity, and that often has ramifications well beyond the borders of their city or country. While we introduce our students to the world through readings and coursework, there are many things that are not easily or adequately conveyed in the classroom. This is where travel and study abroad become important. Some are best understood when experienced, but without the proper preparation and context, they can lack meaning.

We believe that course-based study abroad can provide that balance of personal experience within a context of academic study. "[S]hort-term programs can have a positive impact on the overall development of cross-cultural sensitivity" (Anderson, Lawton, Rexeisen, and Hubbard 2006). The places visited and experiences chosen are determined based on the curriculum and designed to exemplify the concepts presented in the course; they are not simply selected based on their popularity with tourists. That does not mean that you should go to Rome and skip seeing the Trevi Fountain. You can do the popular tourist sites, but you should also ensure that the students see or experience the historical, cultural, and political sites which are most significant for the specific course and country to which you are traveling.

> If you wanted to study Asia and post-colonialism, you could do what we did and travel to Hong Kong after being in China for two weeks. The evidence of colonial influence and the degree of Western influence (from road signs to food) were extremely apparent to our students. Part of the travel itinerary (going to mainland China, then Hong Kong) was done for this shock purpose, while the other part was for the practicality of returning to China after visiting Hong Kong. After being in mainland China for two weeks, the students were very aware of how "British" Hong Kong felt.

We design our coursework and our study abroad itineraries such that students have an understanding of what they will see and can thus better grasp what it means in their own socio-cultural view of the world. In other words, they can build on what they already know to appreciate not only what is there but why it is there and what its existence means. Student understanding is deeper and broader if they have the framework to process new social, political, historical, and economic dynamics as they travel to new destinations. Once students start being able to see the world with a deeper understanding, they begin to see not only how things fit together but why there are differences and how they are important. So, even though course-based study abroad is of shorter duration than the traditional model, students have a context before they go, and they have faculty with them to continue to provide context and direction.

OUR STUDY ABROAD PHILOSOPHY

We believe that students must have both an academic and a cultural preparation before traveling. There must be familiarity with academic material and with what they will experience on the ground and during travel (history, art, music, economics, geography, biology, politics, or whatever the focus of the class is).

We must prepare the students as fully as is practical for what they will be experiencing. This means a semester's worth of coursework immediately preceding the travel. Optimally, students should have at least one course in an academic discipline that will translate directly to the travel curriculum and another multi-disciplinary class to prepare them for the travel experience itself. We discuss in detail what we believe should be covered in these classes in the "What to Teach" chapter, but the design we recommend would have both classes be upper division courses. Making the classes upper division courses means that the students will have had to take the prerequisite courses that cover the basic concepts and terminology of the discipline. You can be reasonably sure that the students in the classes immediately preceding the travel have the necessary background to take on the advanced and more specialized material (both academically and culturally) entailed while abroad. If you want to study social dynamics in a country, students could see the Fellahin in Egypt or the Mayans in Guatemala and without the proper context would just see the poverty and could easily miss the reasons for that poverty. With just an introductory course in sociology, anthropology, or geography, those same students would have been exposed to concepts such as race, ethnicity, culture, identity, and status, and could thus begin to wrestle with the idea that the poverty has causes and what the causes might be.

Not only do students need academic content, but they also require preparation for the culture differences they will encounter. This is where a multi-disciplinary ("travel") class fits into the curriculum. Again, we describe this in more detail in Chapter Four: "What to Teach," but we recommend the use of this class to meet three basic objectives: the introduction to the culture of the destination, taking care of practical issues (i.e., applying for visas, if necessary), and the development of group identity and cohesion among the travelers. This course helps students prepare for the travel through an accelerated "socialization" process. The objective is that students will gain sufficient context before they leave to be able to continue the learning once they hit the ground and not simply be tourists. This class is also the place where practical matters, such as roommate assignments, how to use public transportation, currency, and appropriate attire (among others), are discussed.

Faculty are (and need to be) the linkage mechanism between the course material and the study trip. Faculty are the experts—they should not just turn the trip over to the tour guides—and if they are not the experts, perhaps a course-based study abroad trip is not something they should be doing at this point (see Redden 2010 for a discussion on this)! You should feel as comfortable teaching about the destination as you do in any class you would teach on your normal course rotation. Why is this so important? Students will be introduced to new experiences, cultures, sites, etc. and may not be sure how to make sense of them. And that is where you come in. You must be so comfortable with the material and the destination that you can help interpret the experiences for your students.

CONCLUSION

As our former university president once said, "Our University must be a place where people learn to become world citizens. We earn the title of world citizen by experiencing it firsthand, not just by reading about it in books" (Leos 2004). This is an educational philosophy that we have fully embraced. An appreciation of others' values and institutions increases mutual understanding, enriches individual lives, and prepares citizens and students for work in the global environment. Knowledge of the interdependent world in which we live and work is essential to all citizens. We hope that our students will come to appreciate what the United Nations calls the "common heritage of mankind"—the contributions to knowledge made by the many societies of our globe—to recognize and value cultural pluralism, and to feel comfortable negotiating a multicultural world. With this focus on globalization, we consciously plan and implement our study abroad trips to educate the next generation of scholars and professionals who will carry forward this commitment to international knowledge, teaching, and service. In this text, we provide for you a guide on how to implement these ideas on your own campus.

REFERENCES

Allen, Heather Willis. 2010. "What Shapes Short-Term Study Abroad Experiences? A Comparative Case Study of Students' Motives and Goals." *Journal of Studies in International Education* 14 (5): 452–470.

Anderson, Phil, Leigh Lawton, Richard J. Rexeisen, and Ann C. Hubbard. 2006. "Short-Term Study Abroad and Intercultural Sensitivity: A Pilot Study." *International Journal of Intercultural Relations* 30 (4): 457–469.

Berdan, Stacie Nevadomski, Allan E. Goodman, and Sir Cyril Taylor. 2013. *A Student Guide to Study Abroad*. New York: Institute of International Education.

Bhandari, Rajika and Patricia Chow. 2008. *Open Doors 2008: Report on International Educational Exchange*. New York: Institute of International Education.

Brodin, Jane. 2010. "Education for Global Competencies An EU–Canada Exchange Programme in Higher Education and Training." *Journal of Studies in International Education* 14: 569–584.

Carlson, Jerry S. and Keith F. Widaman. 1988. "The Effects of Study Abroad during College on Attitudes toward Other Cultures." *International Journal of Intercultural Relations* 12: 1–17.

Cook-Anderson, Gretchen. 2012. "Studying Abroad in College Helps Graduates Make More Money and Land Jobs Faster." *Diversity Employers* 43: 11–13.

Donnelly-Smith, Laura. 2009. "Global Learning through Short-Term Study Abroad." *Peer Review* 11 (4): 12–15.

Douglas, Ceasar and Catherine G. Jones-Rikkers. 2001. "Study Abroad Programs and American Student Worldmindedness." *Journal of Teaching in International Business* 13: 55–66.

EducationDynamics, LLC. 2017. Studyabroad.com. Newtown Sq, PA: EducationDynamics, LLC. www.studyabroad.com/ (Accessed September 26, 2018).

Forum on Education Abroad. 2011. *The Forum on Education Abroad Education Abroad Glossary*. Carlisle, PA: The Forum on Education Abroad.

Goodman, Allen E. and Stacie Nevadomski Berdan. 2014. "Every Student Should Study Abroad." *New York Times*, October 17. www.nytimes.com/roomfordebate/2013/10/17/should-more-americans-study-abroad/every-student-should-study-abroad (Accessed September 26, 2018).

Hadis, Benjamin F. 2005. "Why are They Better Students When They Come Back? Determinants of Academic Focusing Gains in the Study Abroad Experience." *Frontiers: The Interdisciplinary Journal of Study Abroad* 11: 57–70.

Hanson, Lori. 2010. "Global Citizenship, Global Health, and the Internationalization of Curriculum: A Study of Transformative Potential." *Journal of Studies in International Education* 14: 70–88.

Lee Christine S., David J. Therriault, and Tracy Linderholm. 2012. "On the Cognitive Benefits of Cultural Experience: Exploring the Relationship between Studying Abroad and Creative Thinking." *Applied Cognitive Psychology* 26: 768–778.

Leos, Patty A. 2004. "The Adventure of Studying Abroad." *The Word Online* (Summer). www.thewordonline.org/summer04/advstudyabr.html (Accessed June 8, 2018).

Lim, Wei Shi, Yong Min Ho, Andrew T.S. Wee, and Junhong Chu. 2016. "The Impact of Study Abroad Programmes on Graduate Employment Outcomes: A Propensity Score Matching Analysis." www.nus.edu.sg/global/docs/The%20Impact%20of%20Study%20Abroad%20on%20Graduates'%20Earnings%2027%20Dec%202016.pdf (Accessed May 17, 2017).

McKeown, Joshua S. 2009. *The First Time Effect: The Impact of Study Abroad on College Student Intellectual Development*. Albany: State University of New York Press.

Redden, Elizabeth. 2010. "The Faculty Role in Study Abroad." *Inside Higher Ed.* www.insidehighered.com/news/2010/06/03/nafsa (Accessed March 16, 2018).

Root, Elizabeth and Anchalee Ngampornchai. 2012. "'I Came Back as a New Human Being': Student Descriptions of Intercultural Competence Acquired Through Education Abroad Experiences." *Journal of Studies in International Education* 17 (5): 513–532.

Spencer, Sarah E. and Kathy Tuma, eds. 2002. *The Guide to Successful Short-Term Programs Abroad*. Washington, DC: NAFSA.

Tarrant, Michael Andrew. 2010. "A Conceptual Framework for Exploring the Role of Studies Abroad in Nurturing Global Citizenship." *Journal of Studies in International Education* 14: 433–451.

Tarrant, Michael A., Donald L. Rubin, and Lee Stoner. 2014. "The Added Value of Study Abroad: Fostering a Global Citizenry." *Journal of Studies in International Education* 8 (2): 141–161.

Thomlison, T. Dean. 1991. *Effects of a Study-Abroad Program on University Students: Toward a Predictive Theory of Intercultural Contact*. Paper presented at the Annual Intercultural and Communication Conference, Miami, FL.

Twombly, Susan B., Mark H. Salisbury, Shannon D. Tumanut, and Paul Klute. 2012. *Study Abroad in a New Global Century: Renewing the Promise, Refining the Purpose, ASHE Higher Education Report*. Hoboken, NJ: John Wiley & Sons.

Van Gyn, Geraldine, Sabine Schuerholz-Lehr, Catherine Caws, and Allison Preece. 2009. "Education for World-Mindedness: Beyond Superficial Notions of Internationalization." *New Directions for Teaching and Learning* 118 (Summer): 25–38.

Wu, Hsiao-ping, Esther Garza, and Norma Guzman. 2015. "International Student's Challenge and Adjustment to College." *Education Research International* 2015: 1–9.

Chapter Two

Before You Say Yes

The prospect of traveling the globe and exploring parts of the world integral to your research and interests can be alluring. And quite frankly, for many faculty the prospect of such travel on your own budget is non-existent. This can make the idea of teaching a study abroad class sound very appealing. But we would caution you against saying yes to such a proposition before giving serious consideration to some key questions.

DO YOU TRULY BELIEVE?

Most faculty are called to pursue a PhD due to their love of an academic discipline, which for most of us has little to nothing to do with international education. And it is virtually unheard of for graduate programs to include instruction (or even discussion) of the role study abroad plays in undergraduate education except in graduate education programs. Therefore, most faculty who participate in study abroad come to it with little training on the countless aspects of the experience. While some faculty take up the mantle of study abroad based on their own desire to travel, others have it somewhat forced upon them by institutional opportunities that may arise. Either way, the most meaningful, truly transformational study abroad experiences, rarely occur without a deep commitment to international education. Given the time, effort, and challenges involved in taking students abroad, before you agree to lead course-based study abroad, it is important to consider your views on international education. Do you believe in (and are you committed to teach) the importance of students going beyond the academic material to place it the context of the history, culture, language, location, and people of the nation or region being examined? Do you believe in the idea of building a better world and global community through education? If so, read on, my friend.

ARE YOU READY?

If you are committed to study abroad and have determined that travel could truly enhance the educational experience, then it is time to consider your role in the endeavor. Before you agree to lead a course-based study abroad class, it is important that you do some introspection and consider whether this is a good fit for you. How do you determine if leading study abroad is right for you? Here are some questions to consider to help you decide.

Have you been approved? The first step in the determination of your leading a course-based study abroad experience will be the approval by your university. The specific office or individual who is responsible for approving you and the overall approval process will vary by institution. But you should expect to have to go through some enhanced approval process which is likely going to require more information and review than that required to teach on the main campus. This may entail you submit information on your driving record and that for a background check. Check with your department chair or Dean about the process on your campus and who is responsible for overseeing the application process. We suggest that you inquire about the approval process as soon as you determine leading a course-based study abroad experience is of interest. The process may take some time, and/or you may discover that you are not eligible for such a role and it is best to discover this before you put significant work into the planning of the course and experience.

Do you have the time for this endeavor? The entire process of creating, recruiting, arranging, conducting, and then concluding a course-based study abroad can easily take over a year. During that time, you will have to spend a minimum of several hours a week working on this project. Do you have time for that? Balancing one's teaching, scholarship, professional service as well as family and real-life demands can be difficult enough. You should consider whether you have the additional time necessary to devote to this activity. If you are in the early stages of your career and are still working on solidifying your teaching and research, then maybe it would be better to wait and do this in a couple of years. If you are juggling family demands such as caring for small children or an elderly parent, perhaps the best thing for you to do is focus your energy on that. Study abroad will be here for you when you are ready!

Do you have the energy? Traveling with students can be one of the most invigorating teaching experiences you will ever have. So much so that we continue to do it over and over. However, it is also exhausting. Just as traveling with small children is more draining than traveling by yourself, the physical demands of traveling with students can be significant. The need to stay with an itinerary created to make the best use of every minute in the educational experience will mean that you will undoubtedly keep to a pace more demanding than that which you would do on your own. Add to that the demands students will place on your "off" time and you are likely to be exhausted. It is therefore critical that you be in good physical (and psychological) health. To put this in perspective, consider this: Can you walk and sightsee in the heat of an Egyptian summer for eight hours and then sit up at night talking with students about their experience? Can you maintain this pace over an extended period of time?

Are you so inclined? It takes a certain personality to lead study-abroad courses **appropriately and successfully**. It's sometimes uncomfortable for us to say, but let's be honest: Not all faculty are cut out to travel with students. The faculty leader needs to be efficient, responsible, good with deadlines, and never late. They need to create the perfect balance between being engaging and approachable for students while also being authoritative and decisive when necessary. If you are that colleague (and admit it, we all have one) who tends to be the last to turn in their documentation or isn't bothered by students playing with their phones during your lecture (or, even worse, is uncomfortable telling students to put down their phone), then study abroad is not a good fit for you. You are the responsible party and the success of the entire experience will rest on your ability to organize and coordinate things efficiently and effectively. If you are regularly late to class or permit students to be, you should fully expect that you will have some very tense minutes at the airport when your group cannot check-in for their flight because several of the students are running late. Additionally, you cannot expect the students to treat the people and places you visit with any more respect than they show in your classroom. So, before you end up in a situation where you are embarrassed because your students are not paying attention or otherwise not being respectful towards someone taking the time to explain their history or culture, ask yourself, "Do I let them behave that way in my classroom?" If you cannot control them in class, you definitely will not have control while traveling. This behavior will not only embarrass you, your institution, and other students, but it also often creates a very negative group dynamic, which other students will come to resent.

Do you understand? There are numerous aspects of the culture, traditions, and history of the places you will visit that we are going to recommend you familiarize yourself with all of which may have little to nothing to do with your academic discipline. From cultural expectations about religious conventions to behavioral expectations, you will need to know what is appropriate, and we will discuss how you can get up to speed. But the real question you need to address before you agree to lead a group of students abroad is do you understand the security conditions in the places you will visit? How safe is your destination? What are the safety considerations specifically? Is it a high crime area? Is there

BEFORE YOU SAY YES

a terrorism threat? We will discuss the use of the U.S. State Department web page more fully in the pre-departure chapter, but know that you can use this site for specific information on your destinations. Not only can they tell you about what types of crime or threats may be relevant, but the site also has useful information about the culture and social expectations of the country. Traveling and sightseeing anywhere can have risks. You just want to be fully aware of the type of issues you may face, so you can not only determine if you want to go but also adequately prepare your students if you do travel. The safety of your group must be the primary consideration.

WHAT COULD GO WRONG?

Have you stopped to consider what could go wrong on your trip? We hate to rain on anyone's parade, but for you to make a fully informed decision about whether you should travel with students you should think about all the problems you might encounter.

Ordinary travel glitches can become significant when it happens to a group: particularly one on a set itinerary. You cannot prevent delayed planes or weather issues which might affect your plans, but you should foresee (and hopefully prevent) other factors which can disrupt or undermine the educational experience you are planning.

Student behavior is probably the most critical factor that you can control which may influence how well the travel goes. Behaviors such as arriving late or not paying attention when you give instructions may be relatively harmless in a traditional classroom, but it may have serious consequences when traveling. It will only take one student to arrive at the airport late to cause a problem for the entire group, as no one can check-in on a group ticket until all are present.

> We once had a student oversleep and arrive at the airport 30 minutes before an international flight. While we all barely managed to make the flight, she arrived wearing shorts and a T-shirt, which were revealing and completely inappropriate for our plans upon arrival. We had to alter our plans once we arrived to give her a chance to change clothes so that we could proceed with our itinerary, delaying us significantly and causing us to miss one event.

Unlike your regular classes, when you travel with students you are with them 24 hours a day and responsible for their behavior during all that time.

BEFORE YOU SAY YES

You should be prepared to have frank conversations with your students about what you expect from them. How will you react if they get drunk while traveling? Or use illegal drugs? Or leave the hotel at night without your knowledge? Or have sex with each other or strangers? These may be uncomfortable topics, but we can promise you, they are issues you may face. We have had colleagues who had students get drunk and cause considerable damage to their hotel. So much so, the entire group was evicted the next day, leaving the instructor the task of dealing with the students and finding new accommodations. Another colleague had a young woman drugged and raped at a pub near their hotel. The woman had been with her classmates all evening and had done nothing inappropriate, but someone had surreptitiously slipped her some type of "date rape" drug (i.e., Rohypnol or ketamine). We once had a young man romance and sleep with three different young women on a trip (two of whom were roommates). When we were informed of what was happening, it was left to the faculty to act as counselors to negotiate the situation, which had become quite a distraction for the entire group as you can imagine. Remember that you are responsible for these young people while traveling and can be held accountable for what happens to them. So, it is best to have serious conversations with the students before traveling, where you explain to them what you expect and what you will do when faced with inappropriate behavior. This will go a long way to preventing issues. Are you ready for these conversations?

Even if student behavior does not rise to the level of jeopardizing the trip, it can create a negative or hostile atmosphere around the group that can undermine your educational goals. Just as in your classroom, if the students are focused on some personality issue or behavior of a couple of the class members, no one will have as positive an experience as if the group was in harmony. Roommate conflicts, perceived injustices, and personality quirks quickly become magnified by close proximity and exhaustion such that it may feel like you are managing a day care when students come and tattle on each other. Are you ready and do you want to have to deal with this?

Another factor to consider is the possibility of you or your students becoming ill or injured while traveling. We raise this for you to consider what you would do. Students may for one reason or another become unable to participate in parts of the itinerary, even if they are not so ill as to require hospitalization. We had one student sprain her ankle on the plane on the way to our destination, and for the rest of the trip, she had issues walking—and that was our primary means of exploring our destination! You should consider how you would oversee taking one student to the doctor, or how you would check on them over the course of the day, while the others continue with the planned activities.

BEFORE YOU SAY YES

> We once had a student who, while traveling in China, claimed that her allergies were so bad that she needed to remain in the hotel, while the rest of the group left for the day's activities. We granted her permission to stay and rest but informed her that she was not to leave the hotel. We then informed the hotel staff that she was ill and asked if they would check on her. We were not two hours into the day's itinerary when the hotel manager called to tell us that the student had attempted to leave the hotel and take a cab to a well-known shopping district. Whether it be sincere illness or just behavioral challenges, you are likely to face conditions which are less than optimal, and you have to consider how you might handle them.

And what if a student becomes very ill? If you have a student hospitalized, you will have to have a faculty member present at all times. Not only do you not want to leave a student alone in the hospital in a foreign country where they may not speak the language or be familiar with the culture, but you may be required to have someone there as an attendant by the hospital. If that is the case, who will be working with the rest of the group?

> We once had a student have a mental breakdown and had to be hospitalized for five days. The hospital required that there be someone with the student 24 hours a day. We had one instructor with her during the day, while a second continued with the itinerary with the rest of the group; a third slept (because they were with the student overnight); and a fourth was working with the university, insurance company, parents, and doctors to ensure that everyone knew what was happening and how we would return the student to the U.S. If we had not been traveling with four faculty members, this situation could have been much worse.

Finally, what would happen if you became ill? Is there someone from your university who is prepared to come and take over the trip?

IS YOUR CAMPUS REALLY READY FOR THIS TRIP?

Let's be honest; there are significant differences across university campuses and cultures. Is yours ready to provide all that you need to have a positive experience? An excellent place to begin this institutional reflection is by familiarizing yourself with the *Standards of Good Practice for Education Abroad* by the

Forum on Education Abroad. The goal of the Forum on Education Abroad is to create standards for study abroad objectives. The *Standards of Good Practice for Education Abroad* themselves "...are intended to be used on an ongoing basis to respond to the practical realities of developing, managing, and assessing education abroad programs" (Whalen 2011). This provides "best practices" and a guide for the questions you need to ask yourself about the readiness of your institution.

To ascertain this information, we suggest you ask other faculty on your campus to tell you about their experiences, not just the study abroad office (or whoever is officially responsible for coordinating these experiences). Remember the study abroad office is filled with individuals who love travel and international experiences and they generally do not have faculty responsibilities. Additionally, on many campuses their office is evaluated by the number of students who study abroad. So, they are inclined by nature and motivation to give you a very positive view of the study abroad process. Ask the other faculty who have done this before. As they describe their experiences listen for indicators of how much institutional support they had. Did faculty plan all their own activities and handle all their own airline, hotel, and transportation planning or was there someone on campus to help? Did they have to recruit all the participants? Was that difficult? How did the university handle collection of the travel fee and registration? Who was responsible for handling the accounting and financials? Was the university prepared with answers to all faculty questions as they arose? Who guided the faculty through the process? Did they have any emergencies or unexpected developments on their trip and did the university provide adequate answers?

You should also ask your colleagues about instances where they may have faced a challenge such as a registration issue or problematic student behavior on the trip. How much support did the university offer? Ask them how they would do things differently if they were to do this trip again. Ask explicitly if the university has ever had to prohibit a student from traveling after having enrolled (and possibly paid) for the travel class and/or whether they have ever had to send a student home. You will want to get a sense of their commitment to your decisions on such issues. This is your opportunity to get an unvarnished perspective on what doing course-based study abroad is like on your campus, so ask as many questions as you can.

Finally, you will want to discuss with other faculty how participation in course-based study abroad is **really** valued on your campus. Is it something that will be valued in your annual evaluation or tenure and promotion efforts? How is it evaluated? How is it viewed by other faculty? Do they appreciate the time and effort it requires or do some consider it fluff which distracts from your research agenda or simply a "vacation"? You need to get a clear sense of the value your institution places on this activity before you spend so much time and effort on it.

CONCLUSION

Before you agree to lead a course-based study abroad trip you have to do your homework. If you agree, you will be the person that the students, their parents, and the university administration will look to in order to ensure the entirety of the course-based study abroad experience goes smoothly. It can be a truly transformative experience for both you and your students, but it is also time consuming and exhausting. So, make sure you understand all the dynamics of the process before you say yes.

CHECKLIST

- ☐ Do you truly believe?
- ☐ Are you ready?
- ☐ Have you been approved?
- ☐ Do you have the time?
- ☐ Do you have the energy?
- ☐ Are you so inclined?
- ☐ Do you understand?
- ☐ What could go wrong?
- ☐ Is your campus really ready for this trip?

REFERENCE

Whalen, Brian J. 2011. "Introduction: Using the Standards of Good Practice to Assess and Improve Education Abroad Programs." In *The Forum on Education Abroad. Standards of Good Practice for Education Abroad* ed. The Forum on Education Abroad. 4th ed. Carlisle, PA: The Forum on Education Abroad, 3–5.

Chapter Three

Planning the Trip

Ibn Battuta, the Persian traveler and historian wrote, "Traveling: it leaves you speechless, then turns you into a storyteller." (Mackintosh 2003). And it is true. We all look forward to traveling and seeing new places, to the adventure that awaits us in new lands, and returning with new experiences that become part of our life's story, but frequently underestimate all that is required before we set out for the trip. Planning is possibly the most important part of a successful trip, especially when you are taking students along for the adventure. Planning the trip can be time consuming and is not the most exciting part of our workload; it entails considering every detail of travel and teaching, but it ensures the stories told upon your return are the ones you hope for.

So, you're thinking about a course-based study abroad trip. If so then the next question is, what do you need to do and when do you need to do it? Don't worry, we are here to help you create a plan for a stress free and enjoyable learning experience, for both faculty and students. But before you begin planning you need to consider many questions:

- What course(s) are you going to teach?
- Where are you going to travel, and why?
- How are you getting there?
- How do you integrate the course and destination?
- What is your timeline?
- How do you plan for the cost of the trip?
- Will you use a third-party provider or do everything yourself?
- How do you choose the right hotel?
- How will you travel within country?
- How will you travel within cities?
- What do you need to know about visiting tourist sites?
- What is a local guide, and do you need one?

- Cash or credit?
- Safety and security
- How will you communicate with your students while traveling?
- Do you need pre-departure meetings?

WHAT COURSE(S) ARE YOU GOING TO TEACH?

While some may approach course-based study abroad as "Where would I like to go and what class can I teach in order to get there?" you really should consider the **course** first. Is the course one that would benefit from a study abroad component or are you going to be simply teaching the exact same course you teach at your home campus just in another country? The destination should not be the reason for the course, nor should it be tangentially related to the course. Study abroad works best when the course (and students!) benefits from and is enhanced by the travel. If there is no pedagogical reason for traveling, then, we hate to say it, don't go. By doing so, you are adding unnecessary expense to students who may already be financially burdened and wasting your time. Make sure the course really needs to study abroad and that the study abroad component is integral to the course.

For example, in a course on the history of World War II, a trip to Normandy provides a very distinct understanding of the difficulties encountered by the Allied troops. Standing on the beaches of Normandy, looking up at the cliffs, the enormity of the challenge of landing on the beach and fighting your way up to solid ground is unquestionable. Once in-land, driving through the countryside even today, it is easy to lose your sense of direction among the hedgerows. As an instructor you can describe the landscape and topography all you want, but only experiencing it will drive home the importance of the location for the success of the invasion of Europe. Being there matters.

Today's students are a generation of visual learners and non-traditional pedagogy has become the norm in modern education (Stokes 2002; Matulich, Papp, and Haytko 2008). Traveling to the foreign country being examined in class provides the active, collaborative, and experiential learning environment that fits the Net Generation learning style (Matulich, Papp, and Haytko 2008, 2). So, if you are considering course-based study abroad, the decision on "where to go and why" can be considered as simply part of the pedagogy of the course and developed in conjunction with the content of the course.

WHERE ARE YOU GOING TO GO, AND WHY?

While almost any course can, theoretically, be taught almost anywhere, you should consider if there is material that would benefit from a hands-on or immersion component and if you have a teaching style that is conducive to course-based study abroad. The most successful classes will be those where the content, destination, and teaching style of the instructor are well aligned. A course-based trip to Paris/France would be ideal for an Art History Course. For example, when teaching an Art History class, it would be enlightening to visit Vétheuil or Giverny, two places where Monet painted, to see how the variations of color due to seasonal and light changes served as a source of inspiration for his paintings. For a course on World War II, International Law, or Human Rights, a course-based trip to Germany, or The Hague would offer numerous locations of importance to enhance the learning experience. Other places and courses that can be a good match are Literature or Shakespeare in England; Apartheid in South Africa; and Colonialism in India, Southeast Asia, or the Middle East. Tanzania, as another example, with its large nature preserves with elephants, lions, wildebeests, etc. would give insight into the complex considerations involved in making environmental policy. In each of the previous examples, there are specific sights that could lend insight into the course material.

Now, just because a course and destination are a good (or perfect) match in terms of course development that does not mean the destination is practical. Sure, if you wanted to study the causes and effects of civil wars in modern states, you COULD travel to Syria or Somalia. You would definitely have unique and powerful learning experiences unavailable on your own campus, but you would also place yourself and the students at significant risk of injury or death. Just because the location would match the course doesn't mean it would be a good place to take students.

So how do you decide if the destination is a good fit for you and your course? First, research the country you are planning to travel to even if you think you know the country well. Find out as much as you can about how to get around, safety, political stability, cultural norms, customs, shopping, money exchange rate, and how easy it is to find restaurants which will appeal to your students (trust us they will not be willing to go native every day!), exchange money, and get minor (or even major) medical care. The *CIA World Factbook* (2016), the *Statesmen's Yearbook*, *Political Handbook of the World* (2019), *Countries of the World and Their Leaders Yearbook* (2019), and the State Department's *U.S. Bilateral Relations Fact Sheets* (2018) all provide basic information to get you up to speed on a country. While these sites are designed for foreign service officials or corporate executives, they are excellent starting points for a broad overview with an analysis of the stability, safety, and political economy of almost any country in the world.

Travel websites are also a good source for general information about traveling safety and logistics, although these are usually geared toward the tourist and may judge sites of interest based on criteria not relevant to your endeavor. Nonetheless,

PLANNING THE TRIP

these websites can be valuable in providing estimates of how much time one should spend at the place, the ease of accessing the site via public transportation, and the best time to visit, etc., all of which may influence your decision as to whether you have selected an appropriate country/location. Country or region travel sites can also be useful starting points for you if you have never visited your potential destination as they can provide the broad scope of possible locations or activities that may be of value to your course.

In addition to the historical and political background of the country, it is important for you to do research on the current political and economic situation of the country. You should not only be concerned with questions of political or economic stability, but you also want to make sure your travel dates do not conflict with any major political or cultural events like elections or holidays which can disrupt travel and cause various sites to be closed. Websites for the newspapers or news services of the country you are interested in can also provide valuable insight into current social, political, economic, and even weather conditions. Cultural institutes, national museums, and tourism centers can also be useful sources of information, although their purpose is to convince you to visit, so they should not be your only source of information. Your destination country's U.S. embassy website can also provide information about the country, travel requirements, legal restrictions, and cultural norms and events. Additionally, the U.S. State Department website will have information concerning the safety of travel and travel warnings, as well as cultural information on virtually all countries.

The U.S. State Department website can also provide information on per diem expenses in every country. You can use this estimate for your budgeting purposes. This information along with details of the historical exchange rate will enable you to prepare your students for how much money they will need, based on the itinerary and length of stay. You should have the students participate in the examination of fluctuations in the exchange rate over time (perhaps as a class activity) so that they develop a sense of what the average exchange has been and what it is likely to be when you visit. This activity also demonstrates to students the significance that changes in the exchange rate may have on the bottom line for the trip. We also suggest that you research bathroom and meal availability in areas where you will be. Clean "Western" toilets can be difficult to find in some places (particularly if you are traveling to Asia), and the lack of facilities can have a tremendous impact on your trip. When looking for places to eat during the day you will want to choose restaurants that are affordable and/or provide plenty of food choices. It is easier for both the faculty and the students if everyone has a choice in food options and price. If you are using a local tour company or a local guide, they should be able to provide information on the availability of both these amenities.

HOW ARE YOU GETTING THERE?

The trip experience begins with the air travel. First, when traveling with students who have never traveled alone or out of the U.S. before, it is important that they travel as a group, so no one gets lost, is late, etc. Since you will have a set itinerary it is important that all the students arrive and are ready to begin your activities at the same time. Sometimes, in the interest of cost, universities will permit students to travel on their own and join the group on the day the tour starts. But there are risks involved with this option that may not prove to be worth it: You don't want to hold up the group for one student, or have the student miss part of the itinerary, because of airline delays, etc. Perhaps more importantly, you are responsible for their safety and security and you want them to travel with you so that you know where everyone is and what is happening with their travel. To ensure you are all on the same flight, price out airline tickets ahead of time, so that you can incorporate that in the fee you charge students. Also, make sure you contact the airline about group travel, group check-in, and group-boarding. This is particularly important if you have a big group so that you can easily maneuver the group through boarding, finding seats, and storing overhead luggage. While we mention the merits of group travel, you have to keep in mind that there are some constraints when traveling as a group. Airlines often require a deposit to hold group tickets even before purchase and will not let the group check-in or board if someone is missing. You would likely not permit part of your group to board (and possibly leave) if you were missing some students, but it is an important consideration. Students will have to make sure they are on time and stay with the group at all times: This is a prelude of what is to come during the entire trip. Also, U.S. airlines usually charge a higher price per ticket if you have a large group. Other than increasing your costs, there is little benefit provided by the airline to you for the privilege of traveling as a group. We still recommend traveling as a group as you can make sure everyone gets to the destination at the same time. If the constraints we mentioned become too onerous, you could consider splitting your group into two or more groups and flying on different airlines (with a faculty member accompanying each group). This does increase the possibility that one or more groups gets delayed, though, instead of just a student or two. The first time we tried this, one group's flight out of our hometown was delayed because of a storm at their first layover which would have made them miss their second layover and delayed their arrival at the destination by at least a day. Quick thinking and hard work on the part of our travel agent, who rebooked the group before they even knew their flight was delayed, resulted in the group arriving at their final destination on time.

At this point, it might be wise to say a few words about the value of a good travel agent. While it may seem in this day and age, no one uses travel agents anymore, but those of us who have the benefit of a great one will tell you: There is no substitute! A good travel agent will be able to provide you with all kinds of information about travel to and in the countries, you are considering. They not only monitor the U.S. State Department country updates, but they also have access to industry specific information which can be important in your planning. They can let you know what the history of airline pricing has been over time, warn you of likely travel issues at certain times of year on certain routes (like weather-based delays at the Dallas/Fort Worth airport in the spring due to tornados) as well as share the experience of their customers with certain hotels, airlines, etc. They also have direct access to the airline websites and personnel (which you will not have if you book on-line) which can prove invaluable if you experience a problem while traveling. Their knowledge of the travel process and all that can come with that, is simply priceless. Our university travel agent, Gail, has been a godsend to us time and time again. She has rebooked flights for us before we were even notified by the airlines that a delay was going to make us miss a connection; she managed to speak to people at the airlines to ensure that we were able to get a ticket on a completely booked flight for a doctor who had to accompany (and sit next to) a student of ours who was ill, and in one case, she even talked a colleague of ours through an alternative, safe driving route to get them home in the midst of widespread tornados, with hourly updates, when all planes were grounded.

The nominal extra cost for a travel agent has proven to be well worth the cost for us and we recommend using their services. Whether you choose to use a travel agent or not, we recommend you travel as a group with your students.

While making sure you all get to your destination is important, making sure it is worth the time, money, and effort once you get there is just as important. We now turn our attention to integrating the curriculum and destination.

HOW DO YOU INTEGRATE THE CURRICULUM INTO THE DESTINATION?

The right combination of itinerary and course material can be incredibly powerful. As such it is important to select your course and study abroad curriculum with the integration of the travel and the curriculum in mind. Once you decide on the course, select the appropriate country or city that will fit best with the course you teach. For example, several years ago we taught an International Law and Human Rights class that traveled to The Hague to observe trials at the International Court of Justice of defendants being tried for crimes against humanity. What better place could there be to see the impact of the global community coming together to implement a set of internationally agreed-upon standards for governmental actions? Think about the history of your discipline, the places or individuals who shaped its development and/or represent seminal concepts in the field. This will often provide a variety of countries and sites to consider.

Your course curriculum, outline, assignments, and reading should highlight and support the travel experience. So, once you have decided on the country, the planning of what cities and sites to visit is crucial for a meaningful and powerful learning experience. There are likely going to be more options than you have time or money for, so you should remember, this is not a sightseeing expedition. You need to select destinations which best exemplify the course concepts. We often teach a section of an Asian politics course on the challenges of a developing economy and how such nations struggle with eco-development and the preservation of natural resources. As part of the course-based travel component, we travel to Ranthambore National Park, India, to visit the wildlife and tiger reserve. Because of the poverty in the area, some local tribes turned to poaching simply to survive. To tackle this problem, The Dhonk Women's Cooperative was created in Sawai Madhopur, a community of Mogya (a tribe of traditional hunters and gatherers) less than a mile from Ranthambore. Divya Shrivastava Khandal created Dhonk to help break the cycle of poaching by offering free vocational training to young Mogya boys and an alternative livelihood for the adults, as well as to preserve traditional artistry as they sell traditional handmade Mogya crafts. By visiting both the tiger reserve and the Dhonk Women's Cooperative, students observe firsthand the challenges of providing legitimate economic opportunity while at the same time preserving natural resources, handing down tradition, and providing training and education. It reconciles traditional creativity respectfully and seeks to create an awareness of values and their expression in traditional crafts.

An alternative approach to destination selection is to decide on a country or region for travel, and then plan the course, if your department has that flexibility. Now we don't mean "hey where do I want to go so what I can teach?" For some academic departments, it may make sense programmatically to have an on-going rotation of courses based on regions of the world. For example, a History, English, or Political Science department may want to ensure it provides opportunities to experience Europe, Latin America, Asia, and Africa over a series of years. If you are setting up a rotation schedule for your department based on region or focus, then you can determine precisely which class on Latin America, for example, would be best for the study abroad activity. Nevertheless, it is still incumbent upon you to ensure that the curriculum leads the itinerary.

PLANNING THE TRIP

Alternatively, most universities have selected topics or some other designation for courses not regularly included in the course rotation which could be used to provide flexibility in course offerings when unique opportunities arise.

Planning the Itinerary

The next step is to start planning the itinerary. Start with the objectives that your travel is supposed to meet. Do you want to see how the daylight changes and affects perceptions of impressionist painters? Do you want to see how architectural changes reflect societal changes? Do you want to see the effect of religion on the politics of a country? Or do you want to understand how different cultures or religions view certain medical procedures? The itinerary should support your course objectives, whatever your academic focus. Before you contact a travel company (discussed in detail later in the chapter), it is a good idea to do some research on the country you plan to visit and so you can develop at least a sense of the itinerary that fits your course. You will need to have a sense of what supporting information about the location you will need to teach and what is available to use for the class before you decide to go somewhere. You are going to have to be able to give context to what the students see. The planning of the itinerary should happen in conjunction with the course planning, the two depend on each other.

The itinerary and the course goals should align for the course-based study abroad to make sense. For example, when teaching a class on developing areas or post-colonialism, travel to the Caribbean and competition in a Model Organization of American States simulation brings to light the economic conditions and the precarious nature of developing areas as well as the need to work within international organizations for smaller states. We are confident that the course content and class assignments will lead your determination of the sites to visit and the itinerary while abroad. The students should have the theoretical and contextual foundation for the course and then the travel provides the opportunity to see the theories and concepts in practice. So, while planning a trip, make the course goals paramount in designing the specific course curriculum and deciding the itinerary.

Now that you have some sense of the places you want to visit, let's turn our attention to food. While planning your trip don't forget to plan into your schedule time to eat. It may sound silly to remind you of this but when you are building the itinerary, you need to consider where students can get something to eat, what choices will be available, and how much time it will take them to get it. Regardless of how much time you THINK you need to get everyone fed, it will probably not be enough. Getting 10–30 students plus faculty fed is like the proverbial herding cats. If you find a place where there are numerous options, the students will spend a surprising amount of time trying to decide which place to choose. The more places, the more dawdling there will be. If there are fewer options, selecting a restaurant will be quicker, but then students may take longer to order. Add to that the time it takes the waitstaff to provide menus and beverages, take orders, place the orders, and then deliver them, and the time it takes to get everyone fed and the meals paid for, and the time factor increases almost exponentially. While this may seem to be a frustrating waste of time, try to consider meals as an important part of the itinerary. The group will need some downtime during the day, and you can use the time to discuss the sites seen and the remaining agenda for the day.

WHAT IS YOUR TIMELINE?

Successful trip planning requires you have a reasonable timeline for everything from planning to execution. A reasonable timeline will enable you to advise students to start planning and saving for a trip if they were interested in going during their undergraduate career. It will also give you sufficient time for all the logistics of curriculum planning, scheduling, and other administrative tasks as well as developing a coherent and comprehensive itinerary. We want to highlight two separate timelines for course-based trips: one for university scheduling and the other to plan a specific trip. Some university departments prepare schedules to fit designated degree plans, and as such require faculty to have courses planned several years in advance. If this is the case at your university, it is a good idea to have a tentative schedule for study abroad trips at least two to three years out to help faculty do advance research into the destinations, plan the courses, advise students, and help them save for a tentative trip early on. The specific itinerary of these future trips does not have to be determined so far ahead of time but a general sense of what country or region of the world to be visited is necessary. This sort of multi-year planning is also important if there are numerous study-abroad opportunities on your campus. Communicating with colleagues in other departments as well as the students about the destinations you have planned for the future will prevent trips competing with each other and provide the greatest opportunity for all. For any given course-based study abroad trip, a year-long planning timeline is recommended. This may sound like a long time but trust us it won't feel that way when you start working and it is essential to make sure that students and faculty have the time to prepare appropriately.

Having a reasonable and realistic timeline is essential to any trip planning. How much time do you need to prepare for the actual trip, "sell" the trip to get enough participation, teach before the trip, and then the trip itself? Easily a year! Why? For

PLANNING THE TRIP

faculty, it gives them time to determine if study abroad is useful for the particular class and decide how to take advantage of those things the travel could provide. It also takes time to coordinate the travel, lodging, on-ground transportation, passports, etc., etc., etc. For students, it gives them time to plan for leaving the country, getting time off from work, coordinating family responsibilities, etc. as well as raising the money, determining how the course and trip fits in their degree program, and taking care of any other pre-travel requirements (vaccinations, language preparation, taking require pre-requisite courses, etc.). So, all this means you will want to give yourself at least a year lead time before actually leading a course-based study abroad trip.

We recommend setting the actual dates of travel for the end of the semester if possible as traveling in May/June or December enables students to fully embrace the experience without the pressure of exams and assignments to return to. Additionally, it will give you the entire semester to cover the course material and prepare the students for travel. We learned this lesson on our first trip to India as the course travel occurred over spring break. Returning from a whirlwind trip on the other side of the world and the jet lag entailed in 27-plus hours of flight time, did not work well for the students or the faculty. Additionally, we only had half a semester to teach the pre-departure material and getting passports, collecting money, etc. had to occur during the previous semester when we lacked the in-class contact with students. We left a couple of days before spring break and returned on the Monday after spring break, so while the class time missed was minimized, both students and faculty had to miss some of their other classes. There was zero recovery time. We retuned in the afternoon of one day and had to be back in class the next. Additionally, the coursework and other activities that faculty and students normally would have done over the break had not been done, which left everyone feeling a bit behind. Also problematic was the time lost in transport. International travel of this distance consumed three of the 10–11 days available. The trip therefore felt rushed and its impact on the rest of the semester was significant. Keep in mind, the timing of the trip can be crucial to the success of the study abroad experience. Rushing through the travel itinerary may not provide enough time for the students to process all that they have seen and learned, and, as such, may not achieve the desired goals.

As we mentioned, traveling at the end of the semester is preferable, particularly if the distance you are traveling is long, as it provides greater flexibility for the length of travel. The planning and travel timeline below (Table 3.1) provides a visual presentation of tasks to be accomplished and their timing based on travel at the end of the spring semester. You can easily shift the timeline to fit the planning schedule for a trip at the end of the fall semester. We have found, however, use of the fall semester less valuable to longer distance trips because of the expectation by many that the trip does not extend over Christmas.

Table 3.1 Planning and Travel Timeline

Semester, Year	Month	To do (Faculty)	To do (Students)
2018	August/ September	<ul><li>Advertise the trip</li><li>Hold 1st Information session for students</li><li>Circulate a to do list (* see the following)</li><li>Encourage students to apply for passports, where needed</li><li>Check your own passport, to determine if the expiration date of current passport is valid until at least six months after completion of travel—if not, begin passport renewal process</li><li>Research on-ground vendors, etc.</li></ul>	<ul><li>Apply for passport, or determine if the expiration date of current passport is valid until at least six months after completion of travel—if not, begin passport renewal process</li><li>Consult with advisor about how study abroad fits in degree plan</li><li>Explore financial needs and opportunities—make inquiries and complete and submit applications</li></ul>
2018	October	<ul><li>2nd and 3rd Information sessions</li><li>Initial deposit due (this guarantees students a spot and demonstrates whether there will be sufficient participation)</li><li>See timeline for visas</li><li>Finalize itinerary</li></ul>	<ul><li>Make initial deposit</li><li>Complete and submit applications for any funding opportunities</li><li>Make sure you have your passport, or determine if the expiration date of current passport is valid until at least six months after completion of travel—if not, begin passport renewal process</li></ul>
2018	November/ December	<ul><li>2nd and 3rd deposits due</li><li>Advise students to register for the courses</li><li>Collect at least half the cost of the trip to ensure you have sufficient money and number of students to go ahead with the trip (according to institutional requirements)</li><li>If the class/trip will not "make" communicate with ALL necessary offices to update records, begin reimbursement of payments made, etc.</li><li>Begin airfare search based on the number of students</li></ul>	<ul><li>Make the course deposits by the due dates</li><li>Register for courses</li><li>Check on progress of funding applications</li></ul>

(Continued)

Semester, Year	Month	To do (Faculty)	To do (Students)
2019	January/ February	• Make necessary payments to providers • Book airfare • Teach class • Apply for visas at the correct time based on country requirements • Collect student forms and emergency contact information	• Attend class • Start preparing for travel
2019	March/ April	• Confirm on-ground logistics with providers • Check international cell phone coverage and notify banks and credit cards of your travel plans • Inform students about cultural norms • Go over what to pack, luggage requirements, etc. with students	• Attend class • Continue preparing for travel • Check international cell phone coverage and notify banks and credit cards of your travel plans • Make packing list
2019	May	• Travel • Articulate public presentation assignment to students for fall semester	• Finishing packing (early May) • Travel and learn

Post-Travel

Semester, Year	Month	To do (Faculty)	To do (Students)
2019	June/July	• Settle financial accounts • Make notes about what sites, locations, and experiences worked or did not work for future reference • Generate reports to university • Schedule student public presentations on trip • Reach out to students to make sure they are reintegrating	• Debrief • Recall memories—continue to process travel experience • Start to prepare for presentation at the start of the fall semester
2019	August/ September	• Review student public presentations on trip	• Talk informally about your experiences to the university community • Make formal public presentations on trip

PLANNING THE TRIP

Speaking of end of the semester travel, we highly recommend that you do NOT assign final grades for the course until you complete the travel. The course grade can be an important incentive for student behavior while traveling and given that the travel is a key component of the course objectives, the grading should not be completed until the course is. Traveling at the end of the semester may, however, entail some administrative issues such as how to handle the grades for spring classes that are considered unfinished (do students simply get incompletes? What if they are graduating or have academic scholarships which might be affected by an incomplete? Etc.). You should visit with the registrar's office, other administrative offices on campus, and your supervisor, to determine how your end of semester travel plans may be accommodated and then at the end of the semester and trip to make sure that all these issues are handled appropriately.

We give every student who expresses an interest in joining us on a course-based study abroad trip a "To Do" list like the following:

---

* FIVE THINGS TO DO TO TAKE THIS COURSE: (DESTINATION) (YEAR)

1. Let us know that you are interested as soon as possible.
2. Apply for a passport. You can download an application at http://travel.state.gov/passport/get/first/first_830.html or get one from any full-service U.S. Post Office.
3. Check with the Financial Aid Office about your financial aid package and how the cost of this course will affect it. The cost will be around $X,XXX.XX.
4. Register for courses in (Semester) (Year) that you need to take to participate in the trip (you will need Dr. XXXX's signature for [Course Name/Number], which is required). You also will need to take at least one of two other classes: (Course Name/Number) or (Course Name/Number 2)
5. Start searching for scholarships and thinking about other ways to help pay for the cost.

Table 3.1 delineates a year-long timeline for planning and execution of the trip, including post-travel work that usually accompanies a trip. Note that for faculty, "the trip" is not over when you return.

Passports and visas are important documents for virtually every travel arrangement. Airlines need passport numbers to book tickets for international travel; so do hotels at check in. Sometimes hotels also ask for visa numbers of

PLANNING THE TRIP

their guests to reserve rooms. If you are working with a travel agency or a third party for on ground travel (to be discussed in detail later in the chapter), they often require passport and visa details of all the students to book hotel rooms, and book airline and train tickets for domestic travel. So, it is a good idea to make sure that students have a passport well in advance and apply for visas at the right time to avoid delays in the process. Even if the students don't end up accompanying you, they will need a passport for any other international travel they might do, or they can always use it as a second form of identification, if nothing else.

Many of our students who have never traveled do not have a passport and don't know how to apply for one or how much time will be needed to acquire one. So, advising students on how to accomplish that is crucial to helping students also take the first step towards an exciting trip and adventure. You will need passport information to make many travel arrangements, and if the students do not get their passport early, you may be delayed in making arrangements—possibly making the trip more expensive or preventing some from participating at all.

Today's universities encourage diversity and often have a significant percentage of their student body made up of international students or those not holding U.S. passports. In our experience, many of these students will be interested in participating in your course-based study abroad experience. Therefore, it is important to check the visa requirements for the country you are traveling to. It is not uncommon that there will be different visa expectations for citizens of different countries. This information is usually easily accessible on official government websites but realize that the varying visa requirements can easily increase the amount of time it takes to be granted a visa, so you should inquire at the outset about the nationality status of any interested student. The application process might also vary depending on the nationality of the student.

HOW LONG, AND HOW MANY?

Ideally, a course-based trip should be long enough for the students to experience and see what they have been learning and reading about.[1] There are many factors that will determine this, such as the distance to the destination country, the cost of travel, the time you can afford to be away, and also what you wish to include in the itinerary. In our experience, the shortest time for a good travel experience with a little bit of cultural immersion is 10 days, and the longest time recommended for a course-based trip is a month. Ten days gives you just enough time to start to feel comfortable in the country, while 30 days will test the limits of how much "group time" everyone can handle. At about a month it hits exhaustion point and after this, students may begin to feel so at home in country that you will have to make extra efforts to ensure that they are still learning and not taking the experience for granted. If you should decide to go longer (30–45 or maybe even 60 days), we suggest you build in some time off/away from the group for yourself. Twenty-four hours a day responsibility becomes intellectually, emotionally, and physically exhausting, and a weekend or even just a day where you can decompress helps avoid burnout from the constant burdens of managing students.

The travel time you need to reach a destination will also affect how much time you spend on ground. You don't want to spend two days traveling each direction and then spend only 10 days total on the trip: Almost half the trip is spent traveling to your destination! The length of the trip will also depend on the itinerary and the places you would like to see. However, the itinerary can be customized to the time you decide for travel. The length of the trip will decide the cost of the trip and vice versa. The longer the trip and travel time, the more expensive the trip will be.

Plan the itinerary keeping in mind what you and your students can cover in a day. That means you will need to consider how long you are going to stay at each site, understanding there will be somewhere you will undoubtedly need more time. Your destination will also influence your itinerary as larger cities may require more commute time due to heavy traffic. Also, remember the itinerary you advertised and recruited on was a promise. Don't promise the trip will include some experience or tour if you are not sure you can do it. Students get excited about seeing the places and doing the events on your itinerary and will be disappointed if they have to miss out on anything.

Finally, we would like to add that you should plan the itinerary in such a way that students are kept busy most of the time. As soon as they arrive, you may feel a desire to rest and let everyone recover from their jetlag but sleeping in will only make it harder to acclimate to the local time. So, while rest and leisure are important, it is also crucial that students start doing things on the itinerary as soon as possible. The pace of the trip also depends on the duration of the trip. Shorter trips will mean less rest and leisure time. If the students are kept busy with a full and meaningful itinerary, they will have a much more fulfilling experience. Having more time off or being on their own, tempts them to explore on their own in ways you might not appreciate, and which can lead to trouble. You can always build in time into your schedule "to be determined on ground" so if students want to explore something you had not planned for you can accommodate it. But too much "downtime" frequently leads to mischief. Additionally, there will be some students who definitely want to get the most out of their money and would like to be on the go all the time, rather than spend time resting. Finally, in some countries, where the students are not very familiar with the language and culture, they would prefer to go places with their faculty, rather than explore alone during this "downtime."

PLANNING THE TRIP

The number of students and faculty traveling are very crucial for the success of a trip. Frequently we see that financial concerns end up determining the appropriate size of the group. That said, the number of student participants should really be determined by how many faculty will travel with the group. There is no magic number of students that will make your trip a success; somewhere between 10 and 25 seems to work well for undergraduate students. Undergraduate students and first-time travelers will need more personal attention from faculty and so a big group of 30 or 40 could easily become unmanageable. Additionally, some students may get lost in the crowd of such a large group and not have the international experience that you intended. The optimum faculty student ratio (which we discuss more fully in the "Responsibility" chapter) should be 1:8/10 students. So, for a group of 20–25 students there should be at least three faculty (preferably of both genders) to help students during the travel. The size of the group and the number of faculty traveling will also have a significant impact on the cost of the trip, so we caution you to give group size significant consideration. The cost implications are laid out in more detail in the Budget chapter.

PLANNING FOR THE COST OF THE TRIP

Also crucial to the planning, execution, and success of the trip is to determine the cost of travel and to have an itinerary very early in the planning process. The first question that students ask when they hear about a trip will be how much and where are we going? And this brings us to an important point about paying for the trip: Our experience indicates the need to set up a payment schedule, with an initial deposit due date far enough in advance to gauge if there is sufficient interest for the class and trip to make. We discuss the payment schedule in detail in Chapter 5, but we should point out that you should make all of the payments non-refundable. If there is a legitimate reason for a student to withdraw from the course/trip you can always refund their money (at least that which has not already been spent on plane tickets, etc. on their behalf). What you don't want is students changing their mind after you have determined the viability of the trip and begun making payment.

It almost goes without saying that the destination, itinerary, the timing, and the duration of the trip will affect your overall cost. Summer in Europe, for example, is the height of the travel season and is significantly much more expensive than other times. On the other hand, Australia and New Zealand are less expensive but the cost of airfare can be substantial. We suggest that you develop a preferred itinerary based on your curriculum for your desired length and time of year and then estimate what that might cost. If it turns out that this is too expensive, you can modify your plan to make it more affordable for your students.

Alternatively, this may be the point where you seek out sources of support for your trip which can lower the cost to the students.

That said, the cost of the trip and its affordability, for the most part will determine student interest. Setting a set price for the trip (which you guarantee will not change) is an important early component of your timeline as it is the key to students starting to save for the trip, registering for the classes, and making the deposits and payments on time. Knowing the cost well in advance is also necessary so that you can add the cost of the trip as a fee for the Travel Experience class. We will discuss the use of a designated course in more detail later, but we recommend collecting the funds for the trip as a course fee for a couple of reasons. First, students may be able to use their financial aid and scholarships towards the travel if it is encompassed in a course fee. Secondly, for administrative purposes, it is easy for the students who are enrolled in the class to be charged for the payments which greatly reduces the time and effort that would otherwise be required of you to collect funds. Those using veteran's benefits to pay for their education may also find it easier to justify the cost of travel and have it covered if it is a course fee.

WILL YOU USE A THIRD-PARTY PROVIDER OR DO EVERYTHING YOURSELF?

You want your students to have a great experience. To ensure that, there are several logistical matters that need to be decided long before you travel. You will want hassle free in-country travel, a comfortable hotel stay, a fixed and known itinerary, guides that speak English well (or are otherwise able to communicate with the group), and perhaps more importantly you want to make sure student needs (such as medical issues) are taken care of. As you seek to accomplish all of this, you will eventually ask the question of whether to use a third-party provider or plan and coordinate the trip yourself.

A travel agent offers advice on destinations, plans itineraries, and makes travel arrangements (including travel insurance). A good agent can save you time and money, and will help you manage most travel problems. Travel agents can often get a hotel room when a hotel is "full" because they have connections and know who to call. Moreover, if you're stranded because of a canceled or delayed flight, a travel agent can get you on another flight, often much faster than the airline.

Going with a third-party provider may thus seem like an easy and logical step, especially when one thinks of how difficult it is to plan for a trip from a distance. On the other hand, you may think that in this day and age, when one can do everything online, preparing a trip will not be that difficult. There are advantages and disadvantages to doing it either way. You can have the most amazing

PLANNING THE TRIP

self-planned trip where everything goes 100% right, or everything might go wrong from the minute you step into the airport. Sometimes, even hiring a third-party provider may not give you the experience you were looking for. In this section, we give you some insights as to what to expect when you choose to go with either option. We have done both.

Even a cursory online search on foreign travel will lead you to travel companies that offer pre-packaged excursions. These companies range from large organizations that specialize in planning educational tours for high school and college classes, to smaller companies/travel agents who will put together a basic itinerary. Some of the largest tour providers have well-established itineraries to offer and provide hotel accommodations, on-ground transportation, entrance to sites, local guides, knowledge of restaurants, and shopping and other areas your students might want to visit, as well as provide continual on-ground representation and assistance. These companies determine the itinerary, etc. before signing up people to join them, so you will have a ready-to-go trip around which you can plan your academic components. This may sound like a dream to faculty since you don't have to worry about those details and can focus on preparing the students and teaching. Going with a third-party can also be the best option for a faculty member leading their first study abroad class or when visiting a country for the first time. However, there can be drawbacks to going with an educational travel company with a pre-determined itinerary.

You need to make sure your tour company is aware that this trip is a part of a course and that the itinerary you have chosen supports your curriculum, therefore you are committed to it occurring as planned. Prior to departure negotiate with the tour company (or whoever is dealing with the on-ground logistics) on all the services offered for the amount that you are paying. Be absolutely clear what you expect from the tour company and stick firmly to your itinerary. You have promised a certain experience to your students and have created an itinerary that integrates the travel with your coursework. Unless you are okay with a substitute site visit suggested by your tour company that maintains the integrity of your travel plans with regard to your curriculum, you must be committed to your itinerary.

Unless you know the on-ground people well, you should try to have some leverage over the company offering the services. There are two primary means of applying leverage: withholding payment and providing negative reviews of the service you received. Problems with the tour company that rise to the level of requiring legal action are beyond our scope and should be referred to the appropriate office at your university.

Most tour companies require at least some deposit paid before travel, while some companies may require 100% to be paid before the date of the travel.

PLANNING THE TRIP

The tour companies will need to make their own deposits to ensure your arrangements, particularly if they handle hotel bookings, entrance to museums, and the like, and so, they will want to have your money to cover these expenses instead of bearing the financial burden until they receive your payment. If you pay 100% of the costs before you travel that would mean that you have lost most leverage over the tour company if they provide unacceptable service or fail to deliver the services they promised. You cannot withhold payment if you have already paid. You are then left with providing negative reviews of their service. This may result in the tour company reaching out to you to provide a resolution that will offset the bad reviews. There is, of course, no guarantee of this and you may just end up with service and an experience that are sub-par. Ultimately, you need to have a clear understanding of what you want and what your tour company can and will provide (i.e., a contract).

When negotiating with tour companies, read the fine print on the contract and the company's website on what your options are if you are unhappy with their work. So, what do you look for? (1) A guarantee that the company will take you to all of the destinations you have built into your curriculum: (2) the housing arrangements are to your specifications; (3) all of the tour company's obligations are their responsibility (so you don't have to pay if they fail to meet a deadline, check-in time, etc.); (4) ALL costs are explicitly stated; (5) tour guides are experts and will perform the tasks you need them to (be sure to include items such as translation services if necessary and help in negotiating the various destinations); (6) the tour company will not only provide the agreed upon services at your destinations, but they have a clearly stated plan for unexpected emergencies (for example, this could include a local assistance network or additional staff who are on call); (7) you should expect that they spell out clearly their plans for the safety and security of your group, have a service philosophy that meets your expectations (do you expect them to be available 24/7 or just during certain hours?); (8) any accommodations can be previewed and an alternative provided if they do not meet your agreed upon criteria; (9) and there is a clear procedure in place for resolving any disagreements over the service and what, if any, compensation you might expect if the tour company fails to meet its agreed upon obligations. It is important to make clear to the company or the tour agent on what your priorities are and that you expect to get what you ordered. Remember this is your trip and you are ultimately responsible for giving the students what you promised them. If you are planning the trip yourself and using local tour companies to provide on-ground logistics, you would ideally pay enough to make the arrangements and then pay the balance once you get to your destination, if not at the conclusion of the trip.

Be sure to do your research when choosing the travel company, as they are not all equal and some of their cost saving strategies may not generate the trip

PLANNING THE TRIP

dynamic you are looking for. Some of the larger organizations not only have pre-established itineraries that may or may not fit well with the focus of your class, but they also are known for combining groups while traveling. While the creation of a larger group can create some economies of scale which provides you an attractive price, it also means that you will be traveling with students who are not in your class and do not necessarily share the academic focus you are hoping to achieve. This can be a good option if you only have a very small group of students and you need the assistance and structure these tour companies may provide but realize you will have little flexibility in the creation of the itinerary and almost no ability to modify plans to fit developments and preferences once you are on-ground. Using a smaller educationally focused organization which builds the itinerary with you based on your course focus and goals can be slightly more expensive but is often worth the extra expense. These companies can provide the same support services as the larger ones (from on-ground transportation to guides and hotels) but provide a more intimate and relevant experience. A well-respected educational tour company can make the travel a breeze while maintaining the particular focus of your class.

We recommend that you try and find a company that someone you know has dealt with in the past. Or if you have a travel company that you successfully used in the past but are traveling to a new country, start by asking them. If they cannot manage the trip to a new area, they are likely to have professional contacts to which they can direct you. If you have little experience, don't know anyone who may have visited the country you are interested in or who used a particular provider, your university study abroad office may be of assistance. They will likely have information on travel agents and tour companies that specialize in educational tours. No matter what type of provider you are considering, make sure to check out the feedback you find on-line about their previous trips and performance. You can sometimes learn a great deal about how these organizations deal with challenges and accommodate various interests in the reviews of previous travelers.

To find the best provider for your expectations and course goals, you will need to research their particular focus or strengths. Check with colleagues, look at ratings, look at sample itineraries, compare what they offer with what you would design for the trip, and contact previous clients. Websites such as www.goabroad.com, www.studyabroad101.com, and www.gooverseas.com/study-abroad have searchable lists of third-party providers with user reviews.

If you decide to plan the itinerary yourself, you will need to consider all aspects of the travel experience. You will have to research all travel, hotel, and on-ground aspects of the trip yourself. If you have someone else plan it, you will need to review all their selections on these topics. So here are some things to take into consideration.

HOW DO YOU CHOOSE THE RIGHT HOTEL?

Selecting the right hotel is a major part of a successful trip. We believe quality lodgings are important because they provide a retreat from the weather, noise, congestion, and the general stress and exhaustion of travel. It allows the students to recuperate from a day that may have challenged them (physically, emotionally, or psychologically) so that they are ready for the next day. Therefore, it is important that you select a hotel that is nice enough to provide students (and you) the opportunity to rest and process the experiences of the day. Many third-party providers have connections or agreements in place with hotels to provide discounted rates and amenities, such as breakfast included, Wi Fi, etc. These can be beneficial, but make sure the hotels they suggest are nice enough for your needs. If you are planning the trip yourself, you will have to find the hotel that is right for your group. Either way, you should consider several things.

Location

The most important factor in selecting a hotel is location. A centrally located hotel with restaurants, shopping, and essentials within walking distance is important, as is access to public transportation if that is being used. A centrally located hotel may save you time getting to the sites on your itinerary, especially if you are near public transportation.

Unfortunately, well located hotels can be quite costly. Cost is a critical consideration in selecting a hotel, but you should try to find a balance between cost and location. Hotel costs are a large component in the overall cost of the trip, so if you select a particularly costly hotel, the trip may become too expensive and end up deterring students' participation. Hotels that have good access to public transportation (some hotels even have their own car service and provide shuttles for group transportation), have shopping and restaurants within 10–15 miles, and are affordable are excellent choices for student groups. Hotels which are a bit further out may be more affordable, but only if they have the transportation you need will they be a good compromise. Lodging costs will also depend on the country you are traveling in, so don't be surprised if you hear that some faculty have been able to house their students in very nice hotels, while you are struggling to find even modest accommodations. For example, hotel costs in India are very affordable, and we have always been able to use 5-star hotel accommodations at good locations for the price of a 2- or 3-star hotel in the U.S. However, hotels in Europe tend to be more expensive and we have had to use budget hotels and hostels (which are not always the most comfortable) to keep costs in check.

PLANNING THE TRIP

Remember that the most convenient location and affordability, while important, are not always enough of a consideration. Be sure to check the area surrounding the accommodations to make sure you do not end up in a seedy or dangerous part of town and that the hotel/hostel is as advertised. Trust us when we say that a sign in each hotel room that states "Coming soon: your phone!" is not the same as actually *having* a phone in every room. And when someone assures you that "no one has ever complained before" doesn't mean that you won't end up in a hotel in the red-light district. And yes, both of these have happened to us.

> When we went to St. Kitts, we chose a hotel based on cost. The cost differential to the best hotel on the island was not much and was easily outweighed by the fact that the hotel we chose had few amenities and even getting to an ATM was a $20.00 taxi ride round trip whereas the best hotel had as wide a range of amenities as anyplace on the island. Price should not always be the deciding factor.

Services

In addition to location and cost, services provided by the hotel should also be an important consideration. Some hotel rates include breakfast, which can be important for students. As the price of lodging should be pre-paid as part of the travel fee, students are guaranteed one solid meal a day, even if they run low on money later. So, if possible, select a nice hotel with good breakfast options. Additionally, while most hotels also have their own restaurants that's not a guarantee and you will want to ensure your hotel has a decent one with hours of operation that can accommodate your schedule. Although, such restaurants can be somewhat expensive, at least the students have access to a restaurant at the hotel premises and won't need to go out to find food late at night or before the day's activities.

Another service of paramount importance to students is free Wi-Fi. It is very common that as soon as we enter the hotel (even before they go to their rooms) students want to use the Wi-Fi to chat with their family or send messages to their friends. Free Wi-Fi is important as it makes them feel at home and connected while in a far-away land. If the hotels charge for Wi-Fi access, expect to have some unhappy students when they start to accumulate unexpected hotel charges. Some hotels charge for Wi-Fi, but that cost can be negotiated when you book a block of rooms. Therefore, we suggest you inquire about this option so that students don't have to pay for it themselves.

PLANNING THE TRIP

Other amenities to look for when selecting a hotel include laundry services, free shuttle service to key sites or areas, hair dryers, or coffee/tea pots in the room, etc. We suggest that you don't simply write these off as luxuries your students don't need or something you expect to be in every hotel. Laundry services can be important during an extended study abroad trip, so the students don't have to carry too many clothes (which will cause luggage weight and transport issues). Most hotels offer laundry services that are very fast but also expensive depending on the type of hotel and country of visit. Nevertheless, it is a good idea to budget for laundry and to inform the students as well. Some students can carry Woolite or other detergent packets to wash small personal items. However, it will be a good idea to check with the hotel on their policy of guests doing laundry in the rooms. Some hotels do not allow laundry in rooms, while others have provisions like the clothes line over the bathtub etc., indicating that they are okay with that. These are questions you can ask the hotel at the time of booking. This may be a minor issue to some but will be a major issue when students complain that they have to pay to do laundry, have no more clean clothes left, or are poorly dressed during travel. The gym, swimming pool, and beauty salon are other amenities and services that make traveling easier for the students as they do not have to go out into an unknown city looking for these services. And trust us: Things you may think are a basic expectation for hotel rooms, like phones, hair dryers, electrical outlets, and even soap, are not always guaranteed. If you want to see unhappiness in your group, use a hotel that only has one hair dryer to be shared across guests when traveling with a large group of young women. You should select the **best** hotel you can afford. And the best usually means the one that has the most service—and is centrally located.

HOW WILL YOU TRAVEL WITHIN COUNTRY?

The next important factor in planning the trip yourself is the issue of travel between cities as well as daily transportation to the different sights on your itinerary. Tour companies often have years of planning experience and have worked out the details of what for them is domestic travel. As such, the planning and cost of domestic airfare, train, bus, or car rental are often included in their price. If you plan this yourself, you have to first decide the best way to travel. Here again, the choice may be one of cost vs. accessibility. In countries like India where all kinds of public transportation are easily available, the hard part is to choose the right mode of travel. Trains are cheaper, but it can also be logistically difficult to get all of your students' tickets in the same compartment (trust us, you do NOT want them spread over the length of the train!). Sometimes boarding large groups onto trains with all the luggage can also be difficult given the short amount of time between stops. Many cities in Europe have very efficient train systems, like the EURail, Eurorail, Eurostar, etc. for which tickets and passes are available online and can be purchased ahead of time, which makes it easier when planning. But note, some countries require you to call and collect tickets physically which will require you to do that once you arrive. Private buses/coaches can be convenient as they operate completely on your schedule but will have to be privately booked specifically for the group, and they may be more expensive and take up valuable time driving if used to cover significant distances. Our advice is to opt for air travel between cities, if you can afford it.

HOW WILL YOU TRAVEL WITHIN THE CITY?

The next issue while planning your own trip will be the travel within a city to the various sights, shops, and restaurants on your itinerary. Whether the size of your group is relatively small (five or six) or fairly large (25), you will want the students to travel together (or at least in big groups) with the faculty so that you can make sure that everyone is safe, getting to where they need to go, and having a good experience. So, planning this will require detailed research on transportation within the city. Public transportation like the subway or local trains can be a challenge, given crowds and difficulty interpreting transportation maps and schedules in another language. Another way of looking at it is that sometimes the challenges can also be adventures for the students and can add to the fun of the trip. Public transportation can also be one of the most cost and time-efficient means of transportation. In Washington, D.C., Berlin, and London we found it much faster to take the metro than to try to drive or bus our students anywhere. But what about cities that do not have a public transit system (or one you probably shouldn't use!)? Bogota, Toronto, Manila, Karachi, and Jakarta are the five largest cities that have no metro transit system (or so inadequate or poorly run that they cannot be trusted). Getting around in any of these cities will require careful planning if you want to avoid spending hours stuck in traffic. This, again, is why you need to know the destination well.

So, how do you determine how to get everyone around? If you book a hotel that is centrally located to all of the sites you intend to visit, you could walk (an option that is becoming required in some places as cities attempt to decrease congestion and pollution by turning roads into pedestrian malls). If you are adventurous, you could try one of the multitudes of alternative modes of "public transportation." These common options, such as taxis, private buses, vans, Uber, Lyft, etc., run frequently, but the ride can be "thrilling," if not (usually) death-defying. And in some areas, they have the reputation for price gouging, theft, or significant risk of being sexually harassed or even assaulted. You have to weigh the risk of these local alternative forms of public transportation versus the amount of time you will save to determine if you should use it.

If all of this sounds a little daunting, particularly if you are going to be traveling to a large city or one with notoriously difficult traffic, you could consider reserving a private bus or coach for your group to use on your daily activities. While the cost may be higher than public transportation or the private options described earlier, you will have all of your group together on a single means of transport, the drivers will take you exactly where you want to go on YOUR schedule, and the pick-up and drop off will be simple. A coach will also allow you to make sure that everyone is together before you leave for your destination or your return; there will be no worry about how to get to your destination (the driver will be responsible for that); and, if necessary, you will be able to leave some items that you need for part of the day on the bus rather than carrying them around with you. Finally, a coach provides the opportunity to use travel time to make announcements, provide reminders, and engage in discussion or teaching.

There is no single best answer for what type of transportation to use other than to know your destination and group of students. Even if you are personally comfortable with different modes of transportation, do your research on the situation in the places you will travel, keeping in mind the logistics of moving a large group of people around. Check travel websites, guidebooks, seek advice from friends and colleagues who may have been to your destination, and travel blogs, being sure to read the reviews submitted by readers/users. You can then weigh the pros and cons of your travel options to choose the best for you and your group. Having this information ahead of time can be crucial to efficient planning.

VISITING TOURIST SITES

Coordinating entrance to sites to be visited is another important factor to consider in your planning. Many monuments, museums, shrines, etc. have entry tickets, which are sometimes available online but in other cases have to be bought on site. Some places do not accept credit or debit cards and require cash. You will need to know this for each site when planning your itinerary, so you can prepare accordingly. Timing your visit to sites is also of utmost importance, since it will help you to coordinate and plan how many sites you can visit in a day. Crowds, access, and hours of operation will influence your visit. Selecting the proper timing of your activities will also be useful, since you will need to plan daily transportation and may opt to hire a bus for the day to get your group to all the places you have planned for the day.

There will be times when the site you want to visit will be unexpectedly overcrowded, or your travel times will be much longer than you thought. Just

PLANNING THE TRIP

remember when you develop your itinerary it is not a race to see how many things you can do. While you may worry about "wasting time" or "not getting your money's worth," realize that too many activities become a blur as you and your students become overwhelmed by new sights and sounds, and exhaustion sets in. Furthermore, if you know travel time will be excessive or it turns out that a destination will be overwhelmed with tourists, use the travel time for discussion or reflection (particularly if you are using a private bus or coach), or find a nearby park, restaurant, or some other place where you can engage in discussion, reflection, and relax. When the crowds thin out a little, then you can bring your group to the site, refreshed, more relaxed, and ready to learn.

Knowing when the sites are open and what the best time to visit is very helpful, so that you can give your group the best experience. For example, it was our experience that the best time to visit the Taj Mahal was in the early morning (at sunrise), before it got too crowded and too hot. We have visited in the afternoon and at midday and found that it gets very crowded and diminishes the experience. The early morning trips allow one to see the Taj Mahal at sunrise and enjoy the tranquility and serenity of this beautiful monument. However, that can be a matter of personal preference. The Taj appears to change color depending on the time of day and the light. There may be an interest in seeing the different colors or you may simply not want to deal with getting your students up and moving before sunrise. Other sites, such as religious sites, may have services or performances throughout the day that you might want to take advantage of. Any local guide/tour company you hire should be able to give recommendations on the best times to visit. So, please keep in mind that timings are of utmost importance when planning visits to various sites.

Another tip when planning is to make note of the weather and climate. Will it be too hot to be outside, too cold, raining, or even too windy for a specific activity? Weather, trust us, can interfere with your itinerary and prevent you from visiting all the sites you planned for your students to see. What happens then? China, Australia, or South Korea is a long way to travel to end up sitting in the hotel because the weather is bad. Do your research and either be prepared to tough out the weather or change the time of your visit. Be flexible. We once had to change the date of our visit to the Tower of London because the Queen was going to be wearing the crown jewels for a state function; and what is the point of visiting the Tower if the crown jewels are not there?

LOCAL GUIDES

A local tour guide is a person who can provide translation services (if necessary) and other assistance as well as detailed information on culture, history, and the general

PLANNING THE TRIP

local environment to tour groups. A local guide normally possesses area-specific qualifications or travel guide licenses often issued and/or recognized by the appropriate local authority. They also usually have local connections to get tickets, make reservations, are aware of the operating hours of sites of interest, and know the locale well enough to figure out alternatives when an unexpected obstacle occurs. Furthermore, they are often residents of the city where they are a local guide and can thus provide insight into a destination that is impossible to obtain without the intimate understanding that comes with the experience of a resident. So, we suggest that you use local guides to assist your group—"even if you are planning the trip yourself."

Tour companies, who help with the on-ground travel, sometimes provide the group with an escort as well as local guides for the duration of the trip. This escort helps with all the travel issues, like checking in at hotels or airports, keeping the group on track for the local transportation, helping with domestic travel, etc. This person also sometimes doubles up as a local guide for certain cities, however in many countries, the tour companies have to use different local guides at every city or state due to licensing requirements. The tour company should make sure that the guide is knowledgeable and gives the group a good tour of the city, while staying cognizant of the needs and interests of the group. A good local guide can make a big difference to the experience of the group.

If you plan the trip on your own, you will have to hire the local guides yourself. Many cities have visitors' bureaus that can recommend qualified individuals. While selecting local guides one must also keep in mind that they must be fluent not only in the local language but also excel in English so that they can communicate with the group. You don't just want a guide with technical or historical knowledge. The guide should also be able to provide a sense of the people and culture of the city. You want someone who is knowledgeable, flexible, and comfortable with college students (who can be a very different crowd than most tourists). Students will always be interested in shopping, nightclubs, etc. and the local guide should be prepared with appropriate and affordable suggestions. A cautionary note: Sometimes, local guides get a commission for bringing tourists and big groups to certain stores, shops, restaurants, etc. You should be aware of this, and make sure they are not taking the group to places that are too expensive or to which students are uninterested just because they get commission.

CASH OR CREDIT?

And while we are on the subject of shuttling about from city to city and site to site, we should talk money for a minute. Throughout your trip you are going to spend a significant amount of money. Now is the time to determine if you are going to bring cash with you and exchange it for the local currency

PLANNING THE TRIP

(the advantages of which we discuss in Chapter Eight, "On Ground"), if you will use an ATM to withdraw money as you need it, if you will put everything on a credit card, or if you will do some combination of the three. No matter what, you will have to do your research on the use of credit and ATM cards in foreign countries. Depending on where you are going, credit card transactions may not be common, so you will then need cash. If that is the case, you have to either bring enough money to meet all of your expenses or make ATM withdrawals. If you don't want to carry so much cash, you will need to make trips to banks or ATM machines (which often means transaction fees). This is not always as easy as we think it will be. Your bank may not have a relationship with the bank that runs the ATM you are trying to use, and your transaction will be declined. So, you look for another, and another, and another until you find one that your bank will accept. Also, realize that not all ATMs are what they appear to be. In South Korea, for example, there are different ATMs for domestic transactions and international transactions. Whether they are solely domestic money dispensers is stated on the ATM—in *Hangul*. If you don't read *Hangul*, you will need to get someone to translate for you or just keep trying until you find one that works.

You should call your own bank first and ask them if you can use your card in the country you will be traveling to and if so, what are fees and conditions associated with doing so. Most ATMs, particularly outside of the U.S. require cards with chips. On a trip to Germany, two faculty lost their ATM cards at the cash machines because the cards had no chips and the ATM did not recognize the password. This later involved several hours of phone calls to banks in America, before they could find a solution to the issue, which involved sending a card through overnight mail. Also, some banks have a limit on daily cash withdrawals. One student had a $300.00 U.S. limit on her card each day, but due to the exchange rate in Europe, she could not get enough for her needs and we had to take her to the cash machine, every day, until she had enough for what she needed. This is important information for both your and the student's planning, so you should convey your findings to the students so that they too can have a backup plan.

RECEIPTS

Before you leave, you also have to make sure you are aware of what receipts and documentation you will need to submit when you reconcile your expenses after travel. Ask your university about what types of purchases or amounts will require documentation. Make sure you save every receipt for payments made in cash or by card. You may be traveling to different places and buying things from small vendors who accept cash payments and do not have receipts to give, so you will also want to keep a registry for non-receipt purchases.

PLANNING THE TRIP

> Once, during a trip to India, we were on a day tour in Delhi, where the temperature was near 120°F. It was very hot, the students were tired, and we had a long wait at the India Gate in the sun. To cool the students, we bought ice cream for the group from a street ice cream vendor, who was quick to sell but had no receipt to offer, nor did he know how to write in English. So, he hand-wrote the receipt in Hindi upon our request, and we had to translate this for the university upon our return. But we had a receipt, and that is what mattered!

It is important that you are alert at all times about saving all the receipts, on payments made on behalf of the students for meals, etc. It is a good idea to carry a special envelope or packet to save receipts so that you have everything on your return in one place and you are not searching for receipts. Be prepared to be the accountant on the trip and keep a daily account of all expenses. This will come in handy as you do your receipts for final submission. Baggage fees and exchange rate receipts will also be required. This last receipt is important since receipts submitted to the institution will have to be converted to the dollar and will require the exchange rate on the day of purchase.

HOW WILL YOU COMMUNICATE WITH YOUR STUDENTS WHILE TRAVELING?

An essential part of planning is to make sure that you can use your cell phones during your travel and in the country you are traveling to. It is important to have access to at least a shared or common cell phone that can be used by faculty to make international phone calls during the trip, since all phones and carriers are not compatible in other countries, and global travel plans can be very expensive. This will become especially critical in the case of an emergency, if you don't have access to a phone. It will be a good idea to invest in a global travel phone plan, at least for the phones that the faculty will carry with them.

Knowing how to make calls home to the U.S. is very important. Both faculty and students should educate themselves on how to make international calls, since it differs from country to country, and it might not be as simple as dialing your loved one back home and might involve substantial costs to make even a three-minute conversation. Some countries use calling cards which can be a bit complicated to use. Once on a trip to China, we attempted to use a phone card where all the instructions were in Chinese and we had to use an interpreter to even translate what the pre-recorded instructions were telling us. It was both

PLANNING THE TRIP

frustrating and comical at the same time. Also, parents may want to get in touch with their children throughout the trip, so knowing how incoming calls will be billed is important as well.

> On one study abroad trip, a parent, not being able to reach her child, called the faculty member demanding to speak to her daughter at 3:30 a.m. The faculty reminded the parent that the student had her own room and that she should be called there but given the demands of the parent the faculty member had to get dressed, find the student's hotel room information, find the room, and wake the student to have her call home. As it turns out, after talking to her mother for several hours earlier that evening, she had simply fallen asleep and not plugged her phone in, so it had no charge and did not ring. All of this drama was because a parent wanted to check on her daughter **THAT INSTANT** and the student's phone was off.

Such instances happen often, leading to a lot of stress and anxiety for you, the students, and the parents. So, you have to inform the students (and by extension their parents) about how they will be able to communicate with their families while traveling. You also have to let the students know the importance of keeping their cell phones "ON" at all times since you may have to get in touch with them.

With advances in global technology it is becoming easier to make phone calls these days. Students can use the hotel Wi-Fi to connect with their family and friends through WhatsApp, Skype, or other applications now available, which can be downloaded on most phones. Choose and inform your students that the group will use one common method of communicating with the students while traveling. In the past we have used WhatsApp or Facebook messenger during our travels. This is inexpensive as it works through Wi-Fi and that way even if they do not have a global calling plan, they can still make phone calls.

If you choose to use a messaging app, make sure it is available in your destination country as some popular apps and even platforms are blocked in some countries (e.g., Facebook and Google). WhatsApp is widely accessible outside of the U.S. and has been used by many study-abroad students. Your students may have other suggestions.

However, you should also alert the students about the possibility that their cell carrier may limit their Wi-Fi access if there are excessive charges from remote locations.

> It took one faculty several months after one trip to figure out why he could not connect to Wi-Fi. He thought it was due to where he was or that he had just selected some obscure option that he couldn't figure out how to turn off, but it was the cell carrier limiting his Wi-Fi access. Their reason was that he had used a lot of data while in Dharamsala, India. Despite having turned on international coverage before the trip and notifying the carrier, they still determined that this was unusual and limited his data usage without notification.

Major wireless companies, like AT&T, T-Mobile, and Verizon, offer several international travel plans, but students should carefully consider the charges for calls, roaming, and data usage. Students should be made aware of overseas cell phone costs. This could be done by requiring them to look up what their carrier charges and report back to the faculty, so you know it has been done or just compile the international phone rates and make that available for students. You should also discuss and explore the option of purchasing a disposable phone in the country of destination. This may be a cheaper option and if it appears as if this is something your students want to do, you will need to make the time to do this shortly after arrival.

INSURANCE AND HEALTH

When planning a trip, we always hope nothing goes wrong and we are able to return without ever having to visit a hospital or even a pharmacy for cold medicine. However, that is rarely the case. For example, we once had to use the hotel doctor to get a prescription for an inhaler for a student who forgot to pack her own, we have had to purchase sunburn relief supplies for students in the Caribbean, and we cannot tell you the number of times we have had to buy medicine for upset stomachs or sore throats. Things happen, but the magnitude and impact of the incident can be minimized if you are prepared, at least with the basic information. It is important to do your research on how their insurance works AND the way hospitals work in the destination country as well as the locations of pharmacies and hospitals near your hotel.

As we mentioned earlier, a critical requirement for any international travel is the purchasing of international health insurance. That said, some may choose to rely on their U.S. domestic health insurance. If you do, you will need to know what your domestic insurance will cover for costs incurred while traveling outside the U.S as well as whether they will pay to fly you home in an emergency.

If you are going to purchase a supplement to your domestic insurance policy or separate international travel insurance, you will need to do so long before you travel because some countries require health insurance prior to issuing you a visa. While the prospect of dealing with health care issues can be daunting, remember that going to a doctor outside of the U.S. is often much more affordable and easily accessible in many countries, even without insurance.

You do need to do some research, however, on the availability and location of hospitals and the level of treatment available, where you will be traveling. Also, inquire as to what kind of payment would be expected (cash or card?), and what documents might be needed. If you are traveling in rural areas and remote locations, doing pre-departure homework on available medical facilities will come in particularly useful if the situation arises. Even knowing about pharmacy locations might be a lifesaver, since in many countries, pharmacies have a resident doctor who can assist with first aid and simple ailments. Your local guide will be able to provide this information for you. Alternatively, you can inquire with the hotels you have selected about whether they have a house doctor and their proximity to medical services.

A Crisis/Emergency Plan

You should also make yourself familiar with your institution's travel abroad emergency or crisis management plan before you leave. A copy of the plan (or at least the basic outlines with the appropriate contact information for those who are responsible at your institution) is one of the items that should be with you and within easy reach throughout the trip. If you have to rush someone to the hospital you want to have all the information on who, when, and how to notify the institution with you. You don't want to have to run back to the hotel to get that information.

In the unlikely event your university does not already have a travel abroad emergency or crisis management plan, you need to develop one in conjunction with the study abroad office and campus attorney. Fortunately, there are plenty of examples and resources available. A simple Internet search for **study + abroad + emergency + management + plan** will give you hits from high school and college study abroad offices from all around the U.S. and the world. While there are variations from school to school, almost all of them draw heavily on models developed by NAFSA and the Peace Corps. NAFSA and the Center for Global Education, California State University at Dominguez Hills have put together three excellent publications that will help you develop an emergency plan that should meet your needs for almost any situation you could ever encounter (or help you evaluate the plans you do have in place). *Crisis Management in*

PLANNING THE TRIP

a Cross-Cultural Setting: International Student and Scholar Services (2017) (which has free, downloadable checkoff sheets for use by faculty and study abroad staff during an emergency) and *Crisis Management for Education Abroad* (2017) can be purchased from the NAFSA shop, at https://www.nafsa.org/ while *SAFETI Adaptation of Peace Corps Resources: Crisis Management Handbook* (2018) can be downloaded for free at http://globaled.us/peacecorps/crisis-management-handbook.asp#3.

PRE-DEPARTURE MEETINGS

Mandatory pre-departure meetings or classes are essential to go over all the logistics of travel. Even if you have the students in a dedicated class, as we discuss in Chapter Four, you should plan to review all the details with the students several times before travel. Students don't always listen and rarely remember everything you say in class, so it is a good idea to keep reminding the students of the most important things (such as when they should meet you at the airport) and prepare handouts outlining what they must pack and reminding them to bring essentials on the plane with them (i.e., passport, visas, and medications). We suggest that you both post that information on your on-line course management system (i.e., Blackboard, WebCT, etc.) and give it to the students ahead of time, so they have it on paper.

CONCLUSION

Preparing every possible detail of the trip is a time-consuming (if not sometimes overwhelming) task but it will all be worth it when everything goes as you hoped for. Students feel less stressed and can focus on the experience, when they see that you have everything under control. Once the students are at ease, they can embrace the differences in culture, the challenges of living in close proximity to their classmates, and the realities of being on the move all the time. Students will be more open to the experiences you have planned and learn more if they are not worried about the logistics of the trip. Even if minor issues arise, students are more likely to be flexible and take it in stride if they can see that the issue was not due to poor planning. A carefully **planned** trip will also allow you to focus on the teaching, learning, and the overall experience of the trip.

CHECKLIST

- [ ] What course(s) are you going to teach?
- [ ] Where to go and why?
- [ ] How are you getting there?

- ☐ Integrating the course and destination
- ☐ Timeline
- ☐ Cost of the trip
- ☐ Use of third-party provider vs. doing it yourself
- ☐ Hotel
- ☐ Travel within country
- ☐ Travel in the city
- ☐ Visiting tourist sites
- ☐ Local guides
- ☐ Cash or credit?
- ☐ Safety and security
- ☐ Cell phones and communicating with your students while traveling
- ☐ Pre-departure meetings

NOTE

1 There is no consensus in the study abroad literature about the optimal length of a course-based study abroad trip. The suggested length of travel ranges from eight days to a semester. See Addleman, Brazo, and Cevallos (2011, 57–58).

REFERENCES

Addleman, Rebecca A., Carol Jo Brazo, and Tatiana Cevallos. 2011. "Transformative Learning through Cultural Immersion." *Northwest Journal of Teacher Education* 9 (1): 55–67.

Albrecht, Teri J., ed. 2015. *Crisis Management in a Cross-Cultural Setting: International Student and Scholar Services*. Washington, DC: NAFSA: Association of International Educators.

Central Intelligence Agency. 2016. *The World Factbook*. Washington, DC: Central Intelligence Agency. www.cia.gov/library/publications/the-world-factbook/index.html (Accessed September 26, 2018).

Heath-Brown, Nicholas. 2019. *Countries of the World & Their Leaders Yearbook*. London: Palgrave Macmillan.

Lansford, Tom. 2017. *Political Handbook of the World*. Washington, DC: CQ Press.

Mackintosh-Smith, Tim, ed. 2003. *The Travels of Ibn Battutah* (Macmillan Collector's Library), new ed. Basingstoke Hampshire, England: Pan Macmillan.

Martin, Patricia C., ed. 2017. *Crisis Management for Education Abroad*. Washington, DC: NAFSA: Association of International Educators.

Matulich, Erica, Raymond Papp, and Diana L. Haytko. 2008. "Continuous Improvement through Teaching Innovations: A Requirement for Today's Learners." *Marketing Education Review* 18 (Spring): 1–6.

Palgrave Macmillan. 2019. *The Statesman's Yearbook 2019: The Politics, Cultures and Economies of the World*. New York: Palgrave Macmillan.

SAFETI Clearinghouse of the Center for Global Education. 2018. *SAFETI Adaptation of Peace Corps Resources: Crisis Management Handbook.* http://globaled.us/peacecorps/crisis-management-handbook.asp#3 (Accessed October 4, 2018).

Stokes, Suzanne. 2002. "Visual Literacy in Teaching and Learning: A Literature Perspective." *Electronic Journal for the Integration of Technology in Education* 1: 10–19.

United States Department of State. 2018. *U.S. Bilateral Relations Fact Sheets.* www.state.gov/r/pa/ei/bgn/ (Accessed September 26, 2018).

Chapter Four

What to Teach

Traveling abroad gives us an opportunity not simply to learn about a new place, culture, or people but to experience it. But understanding that experience is key. Therefore, deciding precisely what material to teach and how to prepare your students (and yourself) is of utmost importance to make sure it is a great experience and that the travel enhances the in-class learning. No matter what the academic focus of the course, having some background knowledge of the country to be visited including its history, culture, politics, language, and economics is necessary prior to traveling. Students need a frame of reference to understand what they are seeing and experiencing while traveling; therefore, this chapter provides guidance on synthesizing course curriculum with country specific materials and activities which provide a context for the course and travel. As you prepare the students for travel, remember it is also important to foster a group of students who will be positive and open-minded, and travel well together.

THE CURRICULUM: WHAT COURSES TO OFFER

The first step in planning a course-based study abroad trip is not to plan the travel, but to carefully plan the curriculum. The academic preparation should start with the basic learning objectives as it would with any course you teach. Are you teaching a class about political development or public policy course which focuses on infrastructure? What do you want your students to know by the end of the class about development or public policy? Include that, as you would with any class, in the development of the curriculum. So far, so good. Now, the next part is to decide what course objectives could be included or enhanced with a study abroad component?

The opportunities for courses with a study abroad component are endless. If you are teaching a theater class, a trip to London and Stratford-upon-Avon to see how Shakespearean plays were staged as well as modern plays in the west end of

WHAT TO TEACH

London would be a perfect way of experiencing stage production. Environmental policy? Travel to Germany to see how they have seamlessly incorporated recycling and renewable energy sources into policy with essentially universal buy-in from the public.

No matter what the academic discipline, the course(s) offered should include some attention to the history, politics, and culture of the country to provide the appropriate context. You know what content is appropriate for the course/discipline of the class you are teaching. As we discuss in Chapter One, how you integrate the travel and the preparation into the course depends on the scope of the course, the objectives, your creativity, and the distance both in miles and culturally.

If it were up to us, we would also recommend that you create a designated course for those traveling. It could be a designated section of a traditional content course which is regularly offered, or it could be a stand-alone course. We prefer a model where students take at least two courses (one traditional content course and one "travel" class) before traveling. We prefer this because this gives the faculty the option to focus on general content for a broad knowledge of the country, as well as preparing the students for the specifics of travel. For example, for a course-based trip to India in May, we offered a 'History of Modern India' course in the fall preceding travel as well as the 'Politics of Asia' course in the spring semester in which we traveled. Students who intended to go on the trip were required to take at least one of these courses. These two classes gave the students a broad and in-depth knowledge of the history, culture, politics, society, and economy of India. At the end of the course, students were able to comprehend and comment intelligently on the changing role of India in the present world order. The scheduling of one class in the fall and one in the spring would meet the course requirement to travel as well as provide flexibility for student schedules. Both of these classes were open to all students, regardless of whether they intended to travel or not. In the spring semester, we also offered a "travel" class which was required for all those going on the trip and was scheduled on Friday afternoons when there were few other courses offered on campus, thus minimizing the course conflicts students might encounter.

The basic idea with the aforementioned model was that the students complete a traditional college course (or two) which gives them the academic context about the country they were going to travel to, as well as provides a foundation upon which to learn the learning objectives entailed in the travel course. They would also take a class specifically designed to prepare them for the travel experience.

Virtually every campus has a designation for courses which are to be offered on a revolving or ad hoc basis such as a "topics" class. Use of a course designation

WHAT TO TEACH

such as this makes it easy to ensure you have the time and space for the supplemental instruction required for travel. This class can focus more intensely on the culture, politics, architecture, art history, etc. of the cities and sites to be visited on the trip. No matter what academic field you are studying, this "travel course" provides the opportunity to simulate as much as possible the immersion one experiences in any society. This also helps to identify the values, norms, and social dynamics students will experience while traveling so that they can consciously be made aware of them and will recognize them when they encounter them. The intention is to ensure students fully understand what they will see and experience on the trip. Additionally, time should be spent preparing the students for the challenges and expectations entailed in international travel. For example, if you were taking students to South Korea for any academic course of study, you would emphasize the cultural importance of respect and hierarchy. Bowing, using your right hand to exchange money (or anything, really), and letting older (male) individuals have the first opportunity to speak is a very different dynamic than U.S. students might expect.

While we generally prefer the model described earlier, where both the "traditional" and "travel" classes are taught prior to traveling, we have also utilized other models. It is very common for study abroad classes to take the form of faculty simply teaching students while abroad. If that is the framework you are using, we still recommend you have numerous pre-departure meetings. And there are things you can do to structure the courses that will maximize the study abroad experience. Here are just a couple of examples of alternative course structures we have used for study abroad.

In Heidelberg, Germany, we offered a six-week course-based trip, with the courses being taught "on ground" and during the travel. The three faculty offered one course each, The Holocaust and Human Rights (History), European Politics (Government), and Rhetoric and Political Leadership (Government), of which the students had to choose two. The schedule was divided between on-ground lecture classes two days a week and travel to historical sites and monuments during the rest of the week. We left students' weekends free to do their own traveling. The students were required to keep up with the assigned readings, participate in class discussions as well as do presentations on topics assigned, in combination with the trips to different cities and historical sites. Once again, the itinerary planned was to get the maximum insight on the topics covered in each of the courses. The itinerary included visits to concentration camps of Dachau and Natzweiler, the European Parliament, the European Court of Human Rights, the Berlin Wall, and Checkpoint Charlie, among many others. The decision on "what to teach" in this case, was very clearly tailored to the country visited and what the best itinerary would be.

In another case, on a month-long trip to India, the trip included a service learning component, and we taught a course while traveling entitled "Human Development in India." The students volunteered in a village on the outskirts of Delhi where they taught summer school to the village children, helping them with English and Math and using play as a way of learning. Our students also developed the curriculum to be taught to the local children. Our students also worked at the village Women's Community Center, where they helped the women with developing crafts to be sold in the local market and also did a training on women's reproductive health and nutrition. At the end of each day, the students had an hour reflection on the day's activities. The students also had to put their experiences in the context of the readings that were assigned to them in the previous semester and write an essay on their experiences. This course-based travel with the service learning gave the students an insight into the opportunities and well-being of the village communities in India and how they were taking advantage of these opportunities to live the life they wanted. Through their work at the school and the community center, the students got a better understanding of life of the ordinary people in a different country and were able to put their own lives into perspective.

THE IMPORTANCE OF THE SUPPLEMENTAL MATERIAL

The course materials are the first insights into the country that students will experience so they are critical and should be first and foremost guided by course objectives. The challenge for you as an instructor may not lie in the selection of a traditional text as the expectation is that if you would cover a concept or idea in your "traditional" on-ground class, it should be included in your course-based study abroad section. It is, however, the supplemental materials provided for the travel group that can have a tremendous impact on the overall learning experience. You want to select supplemental materials, readings, or activities which highlight the importance of course concepts *within the context of the country of travel.* An example from our India class may illustrate. A key component in teaching either the History of India or Indian Politics is the ideal of economic development and its impact on society. Textbooks on either topic will examine the question of how the state has developed from a colony to an emerging power and the importance of various economic industries. They will also provide instruction in the social ramifications of these forces over time and the divisions between rich and poor. But traditional academic discussions of this topic would not necessarily prepare students to understand the realities of major portions of the population living in slums. To bring the personal, political, and societal implications to life, we have used Katherine Boo's novel *Behind the Beautiful Forevers* (2012). The characters not only humanize the realities of poverty and life in the slums but prepare them for a tour of the Dharavi Slums (led by local college students) which we include in the itinerary. We also use of R.K. Laxman's *Malgudi Days* (1982) that gives students an idea of rural village life in India for a juxtaposition and as preparation for our visit to Ranthambore and also working in the village. These two supplemental readings would be perfectly appropriate in a traditional class as well, but their use in the travel class ensures that the concepts come to life and provide context for student experiences while traveling.

ACCULTURATION

One of the primary goals of our "travel" classes is to give the students an opportunity for assimilation into the culture in which they will be traveling. Acculturation has been defined, as "…learning of the ideas, values, conventions, and behavior that characterize a social group. Acculturation is also used to describe the contact between two or more cultural groups…" (Hirsch, Kett, and Trefil 2002, 426). As you prepare the students for travel to another country, it is important to make sure the pre-departure course content adheres to this goal, so that the students are ready for immersion into a different culture. The "traditional" courses give the students a disciplinary education with the country as an object lesson, while the travel experience course (or "travel" class) prepares them on specific cultural aspects of the country they need to understand prior to traveling. The course gives the students an opportunity to explore the culture of the country necessary to provide the context and link the academic study to the experiential learning on-ground. Depending on the discipline and topic of the "traditional" class, material in the "travel" class could cover topics from food to fashion, language and religious differences, and even art and architecture. Additionally, we suggest you let students preview the itinerary through research, readings, and presentations on the sites to be visited and cultural and social expectations and norms, so that they are prepared (and in our experience, more excited) when they actually visit the specific locations. Engaging with the course material prepares the students to be open to the culture and people they will experience and reduce the possibility of culture shock which can lead to intolerance.

TRAVEL KNOWLEDGE

You should also be prepared to teach the students how to travel and the "travel" class is the perfect place for this as the class is limited to those traveling. When

WHAT TO TEACH

we discuss "teaching them how to travel," we are referring to 'travel knowledge' or the information and insight you will have to share with the students such as what to pack, what to carry with them on the plane, what to expect when you go through customs and immigration, and/or how to behave in certain conditions. For some, maybe many, of your students, this will be the first time they have traveled internationally. Alternatively, you may encounter students who have traveled abroad but never traveled in an airplane (Mexico is just a few hours' drive from our campus, so we see this a lot). On the other hand, you may have students who have traveled many times internationally. This means you must prepare for a vast spectrum of experience and knowledge concerning the logistics of international travel.

The information you give has to cater to the novice traveler and provide a framework for the seasoned traveler to understand your expectations. You have to set the tone, especially for the experienced travelers, because they may have only traveled with their parents. This may be a good thing or not. They may think since they are not with parents they are free to do anything they wish. Or if their only experience has been international vacations with parents, they may not immediately grasp the serious nature of an academic trip, the importance of maintaining the schedule of the itinerary, etc. It is up to you to prepare all your students from the most to least experienced for the course-based study abroad travel.

PACKING

Some of the most common mistakes inexperienced travelers make involve packing for the trip. Some will bring too many clothes, others just the wrong clothes. You will want to provide information on how to pack for the specific trip you created. Your itinerary is a good guide to frame this advice. If you are going to be working on an archeological dig, the students will need different clothing than if you will be meeting with elected officials. You have to let the students know that when they are traveling, they represent their university, country, and you, their instructor. As such, everything they do on the trip from what they wear to how they behave will reflect on their country and institution. As you teach them about the country and the culture of the country, you should also have a discussion with the students about appropriate attire, based on the customs and culture of the places to be visited. The way we dress in the U.S. for activities outside in warm temperatures would often be considered inappropriate in other locales. It is up to you to provide the appropriate framework for your students.

In some countries, when visiting a religious site, you are required to wear modest clothing. There can be no sleeveless tops or shorts, you must wear a head

WHAT TO TEACH

covering, you must take off your shoes, and you should not be too loud or may even be expected to maintain silence. Students will have to be told ahead of time and most likely reminded multiple times. Instructors will have to monitor this on the trip so not as to offend or cause problems.

Before a trip we hand out a list to the students on wardrobe expectations titled "What not to wear." This helps the students decide what to pack and bring on the trip. For example, when traveling in Asia, women are told to pack a couple of scarfs, which can double up as a cover-up or a head covering when entering temples and mosques. In parts of the Caribbean (Barbados), camouflage patterned clothing is forbidden. Students are always surprised by this, and we have discovered that, if not forewarned, they may bring such clothing. It is often up to you to monitor the students and make sure that they do not get into situations that cause cultural *faux pas*.

> Of course, even the best laid plans can sometimes go astray. On a trip to Germany and France, we recommended clothing for warmish days and cool nights. We all packed long pants and clothes to layer so that as the 50-degree overnight temperatures warmed up to the 70s and lower 80s during the day we could remove layers and remain comfortable. It ended up being the hottest summer in ages, with highs around 100 degrees for the first three weeks we were there.

On a practical side, you can start by informing the students about what to pack in their carry on for international flights. If you have never spent a total of 27 hours in transit or just 18 hours on a single flight, you have no idea how being prepared can make a difference. Students have to be told how to dress on these potentially long flights. They should pack a light jacket, wear comfortable shoes and socks, and carry some light snacks. The temperature in the flights can be very cold, but you don't want the students to pack a blanket or other bulky item because of luggage weight limitations throughout the rest of the trip. Since carry-on weight limits are very low on some flights, you should explain the importance of having things they absolutely cannot do without in the bag (or bags) that is with them and not in their checked baggage. They will also have to be reminded to carry any medications they will need with them in their carry-on or cabin baggage. Carrying light snacks is also a good idea, as snacks at airports and on planes can be very expensive (and might not be available at all on the plane). A travel pillow is a good investment for long flights, but you might want to counsel students about purchasing an inflatable one to save space

WHAT TO TEACH

while not in use. It is also a good idea to pack chargers for devices, even if they do not use them on the flights, since these are items they do not want lost or even delayed if their luggage does not arrive on time. You will also have to tell the students about carrying valuables in general. It is best to leave expensive jewelry and electronics at home as a rule, but if they bring them, they should be in their carry-on to avoid loss or theft. All this said, you want to emphasize to your students not to bring everything they can think of in their carry-on bag. We once had a student significantly delay the group when going through security in Heathrow airport. He had insisted he was going to need his Xbox while traveling and had it, all its various cords and controllers, as well as a 12-plug surge protector in his carry-on bag. The security personnel were not alone in asking why on earth he needed this on the plane when we saw him unload it all.

You will also need to instruct the students on 'how to' travel once they arrive in country and what to wear and pack for their daily activities. On a typical trip to India, we use all forms of transportation, international and domestic airlines, trains, buses, auto rickshaws and even a ferry in Mumbai. Each form of travel can have very different dynamics which you would want to consider in packing carry-ons vs. checked bags or even determining what to bring on a day outing. Traveling by train in India can be a challenge as the stations are very crowded, and at some stations, the train does not stop for a very long time between stops. So, light and compact luggage, comfortable and closed toed shoes, and modest clothing are the best for such travel. Even on day trips you may want to advise your students to pack a change of clothes, sunscreen, hats, a scarf, etc. depending on the type of activities planned. There is rarely time to go back to the hotel during the day simply because of a wardrobe issue. Going over all this ahead of time will give your students a sense of what to expect and should guide their overall packing. If you explain to them all the places where flip flops or baseball caps (or some other item) will not be appropriate, they may wisely decide to leave them at home, reducing the weight of their luggage and making the overall travel easier.

> We once had the experience of students not listening to our instructions about the day's activities when we were set to visit Old Bailey in London. As this is a working court house, no bags of any size or kind were permitted. Several students brought purses, backpacks, and camera bags because "they wanted them for other times during the day." These students were prohibited from entering and because we had a set tour guide we could not adapt and simply take turns waiting outside with the bags.

WHAT TO TEACH

PASSPORTS AND VISAS

Some part of the "travel" class will undoubtedly have to be used to assist students with obtaining passports and securing visas. Most American students do not have passports. The State Department indicates only 40% of U.S. citizens have passports (https://travel.state.gov/content/travel/en/passports/after/passport-statistics.html). As we mentioned in Chapter Three, it is critical that you let the students know from the first information session you hold that they should apply for their passports ASAP. But you will also want to discuss with your students the meaning and significance of passports and visas in the international community. Don't be surprised if some students simply "get" a passport because you told them to and apply for a visa as instructed with little thought. The role of these documents in demonstrating citizenship and the approval of a nation to travel within their borders will be lost on many students. You should impress on your students the need to keep these documents private and secure as well as the somber behavior expected when producing them to customs or embassy officials. The possible consequences of losing these documents must be expressed to all your students long before you travel.

The visa application process can sometimes be complicated depending on the country of travel and also the citizenship of the student traveling. You can find information on the visa requirements and application process for any country on their embassy and/or consulate websites usually under the heading: Consular Services. Every country has a different process, rules, or time frame, so it is necessary to have this information ahead of time, so that you can explain to your students how the visa process is affected by their passports. Whether the visa process can be done entirely on-line, or hard copies of the forms have to be processed in an embassy, we strongly recommend that you treat the filling out of the application as a class activity. Every time we lead a trip, the visa application process turns out to be challenging for at least a couple of our students. Visa applications often ask questions for which students are unprepared (such as the address of their father's place of employment or whether their parents/grandparents have ever served in the military). If possible, we recommend that you access the form ahead of time and share it with the students, so they will have time to ascertain the information they may need. Then when doing the application together in class, make sure to tell students the significance of submitting the form as, if visas are rejected for any reason—even due to typographical mistakes—they will have to reapply, and that generates additional screening as they would be considered to have been "previously denied a visa to travel." This is especially true if they are completing the form on-line. Don't let anyone hit "submit" until you know all their answers are accurate!

WHAT TO TEACH

BEHAVIORAL EXPECTATIONS

As the faculty leader, you have to set clear behavioral expectations for your students early on and your "travel" class is where this should happen. You are the person the hotels, guides, and others will expect to be in control of and responsible for the group's behavior, so the sooner the students understand your expectations and the rules for the trip, the better it will be for everyone. This is not to say you have to take all the fun out of the trip, but let your students know that the better behaved everyone is on the trip, the more organized it stays and the more everyone will be able to enjoy the itinerary. "Be on time" is the first rule to set. Students have to be respectful of everyone on the trip and being on time, and not keep the group waiting is one critical way to ensure that. You are not going to be able to permit some students to move ahead with the itinerary if some of the others have wandered off—everyone will have to wait until you find them, and you are likely to miss out on other of the day's activities. So, respecting each other by respecting the time frames you set up will be very important. An easy way to instill this dynamic in the group is by being very serious about the start and use of your class time. Not permitting students to arrive late to class will go a long way to show them you are serious about this.

Following the instructions of the faculty leaders is also of prime importance and again you can model this behavior in your classes. Every day on the trip, you will find yourself constantly giving directions about all kinds of things—like where to meet after leaving a site, how much time they will have at a site, what form of ID/payment may be accepted at an upcoming event, etc. When the group listens to instructions, the itinerary moves more smoothly. When they don't, you can end up with an on-going sense of chaos that causes delays and irritation. So, you might want to consider how you treat this behavior in your classes beforehand.

We also suggest that you discuss in class the etiquette of plane travel. You will want your students to behave on flights, to be respectful of other passengers, not to talk in a loud voice and disturb other passengers, not to hang out in the aisles near their friends if they are not seated together, etc. A good idea is to have all students wear a university T-shirt or colors so that they can be easily sighted and identified. We have taken to purchasing university polo shirts for the group with some special trip designation embroidered on them both as a keepsake and required attire for the international components of our trip. This helps ensure that the students look somewhat professional, makes them easy to find in the airport, AND helps the airline staff recognize that you are a group. It will not take long for most observers to recognize you are responsible for the group but being visibly associated can have benefits. Some airlines allow groups to pre-board, it is easier for you to find them inside the plane if you need to talk to them, and it often reminds students that their behavior is a reflection on the entire group.

WHAT TO TEACH

You also need to make the students aware of cultural expectations as they travel through the country, cities, and sites selected. For example, while smoking is acceptable in most of Europe, it might not be appropriate in public places in other countries. Smoking is often strictly prohibited (and strictly enforced) at monuments and religious sites, and students should be aware of the cultural views and norms concerning such behavior. Drinking, volume of conversations, and even running can be problematic in some spaces so you will need to prepare (and remind) students to be considerate of the local norms. You will even find yourself telling the students to stay together and not get distracted while maneuvering through large crowds once you get in the country. So, you should discuss the importance of keeping an eye out for each other and staying with the group in your "travel" class before they are distracted by the local sights and when they may actually be listening to you.

You should also use class time to discuss your rules and expectations for their personal behavior on the trip. You should never expect that students will know, accept, or even understand your expectations for their behavior without explicit discussion. While you may not be able to imagine that anyone would need to be told not to change their clothes in the aisle of an airplane (dropping their pants and startling the little old lady sitting next to them), trust us on this, they really might need to be told this! Personal behavior can include all kinds of things. Have a frank conversation with the students concerning things they may be hoping to do as well as things you are terrified they might do. If you are unsure what to discuss, ask yourself if you are okay with them going out to nightclubs, etc. without you? Do they need to let you know where they are going or when they return? Can they go out alone? What are the rules/expectations about their sexual behavior on the trip? Are you okay if they buy/sell/use drugs on the trip (even in cases where they may be legal in the host country but not in the U.S., or vice versa)? And do they understand the cultural norms of the host country on these activities? The point is to emphasize to students that they are representing their institution and the U.S. in everything they do. Good or bad, their actions will reflect on your university and you personally. Everything they do during the trip as they are being observed by others is what the local citizenry will come to know as the U.S. or your institution's behavior. Overall students should understand to be on their best behavior at all times, so make sure you are clear on this in class!

OTHER IMPORTANT ISSUES

One of the most important things you can do to ensure the success of the trip is to know your students before you travel—and make sure they know you.

This should be one of the primary goals of the "travel" class. The students have to be comfortable with you as a faculty leader. You want them to know your expectations but also feel comfortable with you to ask questions or tell you when something is wrong. The "travel" class meetings are a good opportunity to get to know the students and build a rapport. It is also important to build a positive group dynamic before you travel (don't expect it to develop on the trip; there may well be too many petty issues for the whole group to bond during travel). As such, you have to start creating these relationships during the semester, both in and out of class. You can do that by arranging out of class activities, like a meal at a restaurant or a movie, so that you can observe the students and their interactions in a setting other than a classroom. As your group will be the outsiders, expect that you will be very visible, and students will begin to notice others watching them. Therefore, they can become uncomfortable when uncertain as to how to behave. As such, the presence of the faculty leader and classmates they trust can instill a sense of confidence.

Different countries have different table manners and dining expectations. And going out to eat will be a major component of travel and be a time when your group is most visible. Take time in your "travel" class to discuss food traditions in your host country, their comfort in trying new things, AND to review table manners. Whether you are a stickler for table manners or not, knowing how to behave at a nice meal is an important skill. We are not really talking about knowing which fork to use, but rather how to behave as a guest. Students should see themselves as guests in another country and seek to not offend anyone through their treatment of waitstaff and/or their general behavior. For example, we usually encourage students to try the food of the country, before they travel, to give them the taste of the food. This can also be a teaching moment which can be important for their future. Discuss with them how they should handle the situation of being served something they really don't want to try or don't like. We have found that many students have not been exposed to different dining etiquettes and often are quite intimidated.

Discuss with your students that table manners differ widely around the world and that what would be considered perfectly acceptable in the U.S. might be considered awkward or exceptionally rude elsewhere. For example, in Korea, no one eats until the eldest person at the table starts to eat, while in Kenya, refusing a cup of tea offered to you is considered to be not just rude but hostile. You don't have to do much more than take a small sip, but you must accept the offer. In Mexico, eating, particularly tacos, is done with your hands, while in Chile, you should use utensils for everything (even French fries!). In our increasingly globalized world eating together is one universal and a good way to develop close relationships. At the very least, it shows an awareness and courtesy for a

WHAT TO TEACH

country's customs. You will want to prepare the students for both your and the host nation's norms and expectations.

It is common for your travel company or a host institution to arrange for one or two formal dinners (a welcome dinner and a farewell dinner), and a few meals in different cities, possibly attended by the company director or host. At these dinners you should expect that the host will take the opportunity to show off traditional dishes and other food items important to their culture. So, you will want your students to be very courteous and respectful of the food that is served as well as their host. Students should be told that it is not appropriate to refuse what is served or fail to engage in conversation with the host—for however long the meal may take. Sometimes food left on the plate can be taken as a sign that the person did not like the food and sometimes "cleaning your plate" can be seen as a sign your host did not feed you sufficiently and they will be embarrassed. So, it is a good idea to become familiar with basic dining etiquette.

> In India, at a welcome dinner, the students were taken to a very traditional and old historical restaurant. The food started with five to six appetizers, and then two or three items as entrées with accompanying Biryani and Naan (bread) ending with dessert. For the bread and appetizers, you are expected to use your fingers to eat. At the end of the meal, we were given a small bowl with warm water and a slice of lemon, the 'finger bowl,' to wash our soiled fingers in. Many students had never seen a finger bowl and did not know what to do with it. Some even thought that it was for them to drink. Luckily, most simply looked around in a moment of confusion, waiting for someone to start first. There was a collective sigh of relief when they saw the instructors rinsing their fingers and grasped the purpose of the bowl. This was a moment of cultural learning!!

Use your time in the "travel" class to go over appropriate attire for the culture you are visiting! Make sure to emphasize the types of activities you are doing, the locations to be visited (churches, etc.), and that students are representatives of the university (as well as the U.S.), so they have to dress appropriately. Just because others are going topless on the beach, for example, does not mean the students should do so. Even something as simple as what to wear over their swim suit or workout attire as they walk through the hotel lobby should be covered. It is not uncommon for students to have little experience with the formality of nice hotels (or even modest ones) which have expectations for appropriate attire.

Being scantily clad may not only yield disparaging looks from the management and other guests, it can also generate unwanted attention.

Expect to remind students, every evening, what to wear for the next day's program as the requirements may often shift based on where you are going and the type of activities you will engage in. Visits to religious sites might require a head scarf or a jacket, or even longer dresses for girls. Some religious sites, like temples and mosques, do not allow foreigners to go in with bare arms and legs, no matter the outside temperature. Other activities, such as walking up to a hilltop fort or spending the day walking the halls of Congress, may require special consideration of footwear. Visiting a parliament or an official building may require them to be in business or formal attire. Even T-shirts with logos or sayings, which are commonplace in the U.S., may be considered inappropriate for certain locations. You should also discuss the appropriateness of wearing hats or hoodies in airports, camouflage in some places, etc. International locations with heightened security concerns may not permit wearing of this attire. We find that students are always surprised to learn this and, if not advised, will likely not think twice about wearing them for travel as 'traveling in comfort' will be the foremost thing on their minds.

> While visiting the largest mosque in India, the Jumma Masjid, every woman not only had to wear a head scarf, but also wear a cover-up supplied by the mosque in polyester cloth with big floral prints, in bright colors. And men in shorts had to wear a sarong, a piece of clothing that consists of a loose-fitting strip of cloth wrapped around the lower part of the body. Both were very uncomfortable, since it was very hot (110 degrees), but that was the rule, and everyone had to comply. It was also disconcerting that the guards at the gate yelled at the girls to make sure that they went in only with the cover-ups.

This example served as a lesson for future trips, as it demonstrated how important it was to be aware of cultural expectations. This also made all our students (male and female) consider what it would feel like if they had to wear a 'burqa.' The cover-up required was not actually a burqa but had the effect of a mandated conservative garment on the girls, most of whom felt uncomfortable having to wear it. This experience later led to a discussion on gender roles in different cultures and provided us with an example to use in the "travel" class and prepare the students for these cultural and religious expectations.

WHAT TO TEACH

WHY THE ACADEMIC PREPARATION BEFORE TRAVEL IS SO IMPORTANT

Getting the students ready for travel both academically and culturally is crucial to the success of the trip. Preparing the students academically, with the knowledge of the history, politics, economy, society, and culture of the country they will be traveling to, is the foundation of a successful trip. This will allow the students to approach the travel with confidence when they are faced with cultural and language differences. The course materials, discussions, presentations, and readings will enhance student understanding of what they are seeing and help them to enjoy it.

> At a meeting, one of our alumni, who traveled with us to several places during her college career, was sharing her experiences. She mentioned how the course-based trip was more organized and disciplined than the other trips that she went on. She said that the readings and the coursework provided the students a level of preparedness and knowledge of the culture so that she felt that she knew a lot about what she was seeing and experiencing.

The purpose of a course-based study abroad is not only for the students to learn, but for them to bring back to campus the new knowledge and insights. Therefore, an important component to think about when preparing your courses is an activity or some way to formally share your student experiences on your return. We have found that it is a good idea to build into the class the opportunity for students to do a public presentation upon returning. During the "travel" class, students are assigned (or select) topics that they will present to the university community after their trip. This not only builds enthusiasm for the presentation, since they do the research during their trip, take pictures, and talk to people, but also becomes an opportunity for the students to examine what they saw and experienced. The reflection on their experiences and integration of their academic material is a key component of the learning process and not something we can expect to occur without some formal structure to facilitate it. The public presentation can have benefits beyond those experienced by your students. Those who were unable to go on the trip can hear the stories and lessons learned directly from other students. Additionally, it gives you an opportunity to highlight the importance of the academic aspect of study abroad (and dispel the ideas of naysayers). It also serves to increase awareness, interest, and support for any future trips you may be considering.

The course material and the academic content that you chose to prepare the students for travel should also prepare them for dealing with reintegration issues if they occur. The longer the travel, the harder it is for the students to return and reintegrate with life back in their home country. Coming home can be a letdown and they will definitely see "home" through new eyes. Preparing students for the return and readjusting may be particularly important for the first-time traveler since the impact of that experience will also be greater for them. This may depend on how the students are affected by the different cultures and the sites they experience. Students get affected in many ways during such a trip, which continues long after their travel. During a visit to the largest slum in Asia, the students experienced the hard poverty and the frugality of life firsthand. Returning to the U.S. and seeing it as the land of wealth and consumption was challenging for some. As such, international travel can be transformative. Some students grow and discover things about themselves as well as the rest of the world, so when they come back to familiar places, they often view life differently. Given this, students might need help re-integrating. The course content should include time to explain (prior to travel) how their worldview and understanding will change after this travel experience. It should also include some material which directly addresses the comparisons they see and understand that multiple viewpoints are good aspects of learning. In this case, travel blogs can help them see different perspectives of other travelers to similar destinations. Discussions at the end of the trip to help students process the experience and reflect on how it informs their life can also be valuable. The faculty member (who experienced the same things they did on the trip) often becomes the person students approach in dealing with reintegration. Try and be there for the students. A reunion party or some other post-trip get together can help students come together one more time to relive their experiences and discuss life back at home.

CONCLUSION

As you can see, the academic preparation before travel is most crucial for a course-based study abroad trip. The courses/material help students understand the most important elements of the country that they will be traveling to and the main objectives of the trip. What you teach should not be limited to the traditional course material but should include most of everything that you and the students will need to know before they travel as well as prepare them for their return. Keep in mind that you are taking a group of young people on an exciting adventure, and the information you give them in class will open their minds and hearts to a fulfilling and great learning experience.

WHAT TO TEACH

CHECKLIST

- [ ] The curriculum: what courses to offer
- [ ] Acculturation
- [ ] Travel knowledge
- [ ] Packing
- [ ] Passports and visas
- [ ] Behavioral expectations
- [ ] Other important issues
- [ ] Why the academic preparation before travel is so important

REFERENCES

Boo, Katherine. 2012. *Behind the Beautiful Forevers: Life, Death, and Hope in a Mumbai Undercity.* New York: Random House.

Hirsch, Eric Donald, Joseph F. Kett, James S. Trefil. 2002. *The New Dictionary of Cultural Literacy.* New York: Houghton Mifflin Publishing Company.

Narayan, R.K. 1982. *Malgudi Days.* New York: Penguin Books.

Chapter Five

The Budget

The budget is easily the most important part of the planning process. Get it right, and you will be able to do all the things you were hoping to. Get it wrong and the results could be disastrous. In this chapter, we discuss how to determine just how much money you will need for the trip as well as what your students will need to budget.

You will want to thoroughly consider and budget for all your costs with the goal of creating a trip that is affordable for students, appropriate and supportive of the curriculum, and the number of unexpected expenses are minimized. Even if you are lucky enough to work in an institution with incredible support for faculty new to study abroad and you do not have to determine the budget by yourself, it is important that you explore the costs of your proposed trip. You need to have a full understanding of the costs of your trip, if nothing else so you can explain it to the prospective students.

So, what should you include in your budget? (Everything!):

- Tour company
- Airfare
- Hotel/accommodations
- On-ground transportation
- Meals
- Travel/medical insurance
- Passports and visas
- Entrance to museums, sites, etc.
- Tips
- The unexpected

THE BUDGET

COSTS

Use of a Tour Company

There are plenty of options for assisting you with the planning of your in-country itinerary, hotel, travel, and site access. Some tour companies can book your group air travel as well. As we discussed in Chapter Three, we recommend the use of a well-respected educational tour company that will tailor the trip precisely to your curriculum and desired itinerary. A good tour company can arrange for all aspects of your experience, from airport pickup to ground transportation, hotels, local guides, and entrance to sites. The creation of a package with a tour operator can take a significant amount of the guesswork out of planning your budget. They will develop an itinerary based on your specifications and set a price per student as well as a separate price for faculty. (The price for faculty and students can differ as traditionally faculty have single rooms in the hotels and may not benefit from student discount rates at museums and other locations you may visit). The key to the successful use of a tour operator lies in the communication. Make sure you inquire about all aspects of the experience they will provide and make sure you are clear about your expectations.

Whether you decide to plan the trip entirely on your own or use a tour company, each of the various aspects of your trip (from hotel choice to entrance to sites) will still require your consideration. The primary consideration should be curricular, so you will want to go with the option that provides the best experience to support the coursework.

Airline Costs

Air travel (both international and within country) is often one of the largest components of the budget and it can also be the most difficult to predict. You are going to have to base your budget on an *estimation* of your airline costs. The recruitment time required ahead of the date of travel means that you will end up talking about the price of the trip (and the embedded cost of air travel) long before you will purchase tickets. Therefore, it is important that you speak to the airlines directly (or let your travel agent do so) and do not base your cost estimate on prices listed on airline websites. The prices found on-line may not be available for groups and this will be particularly true for the lowest fares. In fact, many airlines charge an additional per ticket fee on groups over a certain size. Most U.S. carriers consider groups over nine as sufficient to warrant the extra fee. As we mentioned in the Planning chapter, this is where an experienced travel agent comes in handy. They should be able to provide a sense of average prices to your destination at any given time of year or give you an idea of upcoming changes or fare increases that could affect your trip.

When determining the airline cost to include in your overall budget, we recommend that you get quotes from a couple of different carriers, then use an average of their costs (or at least not use the cheapest fare listed). We also suggest you add a couple of hundred dollars to that price before including it in your calculations. This should offset any marginal cost increases that may occur in the time frame between you doing the research and actually buying the tickets. If you manage to spend less than you expected, you can always refund the money to students or spend the difference on student meals, etc. while traveling.

As we discussed in the previous chapter, having all your students travel together is advisable. Additionally, the cost of the airfare is best included in the advertised price of your trip. Students are often inexperienced in planning travel (especially international travel) so providing the most accurate estimate of the full cost of participation is necessary to avoid issues of insufficient funds and by including the airfare costs you will guarantee they travel with you.

Excess Baggage

Travel between cities or countries incorporated within your excursion may require the use of regional or smaller airlines. You should check these airlines beforehand for luggage allowances, seat assignments availability (some airlines charge for seat assignments prior to the day of the flight), services offered, etc. On most international flights, there is a 50-pound weight limit on bags; airlines differ as to whether one or two checked bags are included in the price, and there are often significant fees for additional or over-weight bags (see Table 5.1).

Many regional or non-U.S. domestic airlines have luggage size and weight limits (including handheld luggage), which can be significantly less than those on international flights/carriers. They often also limit checked bags to one per person. This means the suitcase(s) you brought that were okay for the international leg of

Table 5.1 Baggage Allowances—U.S.-Based Airlines

Airline	Baggage Allowance Included In Ticket	Weight Allowance (lbs)	Price for Extra Weight ($)
American	0 ($25 first bag $100 second bag)	50	100
British Airways	1 ($79 for second bag)	50	100
Delta	1 ($75 for second bag)	50	100
United	1 ($100 for second bag)	50	200

THE BUDGET

Table 5.2 Baggage Allowances—Regional/Non-U.S.-Based Airlines

Airline	Baggage Allowance Included In Ticket	Weight Allowance	Price for Extra Weight
Air India	1 bag	25kg (55.1 lbs)	$7 U.S. per 2 lbs[a]
Spice Jet	1 bag	15 kg (33 lbs)	$3.95 U.S. per 2 lbs[a]
Ryan Air	0 (1 bag = $33 US to check)	20 kg (44 lbs)	$14 U.S. per 2lbs[a]
Easy Jet	0 (1 bag = $17–40 US to check)	20 kg (44 lbs)	$15.75 U.S. per 6 lbs[a]
Bangkok Airways	1 bag	20 kg (44 lbs)	$3 U.S. per 2 lbs[a]

[a] This is the required increment for purchasing additional weight allowances.

travel may end up costing an extra fee on these flights, even if they are not heavy. Therefore, thorough examination of the baggage fees for all airlines to be used is recommended and this calculation should be included in the overall fee charged to students (see Table 5.2).

These regional airlines are also more likely to treat your group as a single entity upon check in. That means they will simply take all the checked bags and carry-ons and weigh them, then assess the group an additional baggage fee. Even though it may be easier for you to have each student check in individually and pay their own baggage fees, the airline may not permit this if you are traveling on a group ticket. More than once, our groups have been asked to pay hundreds of dollars in excess baggage fees on flights within our host country. The time pressures at the airport and the difficulty in determining just which bag was over-weight and by how much (and thus generating the percentage of the excess bag fee) can make it impractical or downright impossible to individually assess students a particular fee for their bag. Some airlines will permit pre-purchasing of excess baggage allotment for the group on-line prior to travel at a discounted rate. This can save your group a significant amount of money, but it will require that you coordinate the weighing of each individual's bags prior to heading to the airport to determine how much over the weight limit each bag may be and how much each student may owe in overage fees. No matter what, you will need to determine how you will deal with these cases ahead of time **and** discuss them with your students.

Your carry-on bags will not be exempt from weight limits on many airlines. Students when faced with the luggage limitations and fees for check-in baggage will often try to stuff the extra weight in their carry-on bags. But some budget airlines in foreign countries also have size and weight limit for carry-on luggage

(7 kg in India, etc.), and they sometimes will weigh the carry-on bags. If the carry-ons are found to be over-weight, the airline may mandate that the bag be checked in and the fee for checking a bag be paid. This can then add to the last-minute excess baggage fees that the students (and you) did not foresee, so check out your airline website for all their baggage fees.

Hotel Accommodations

As we mentioned in the Planning chapter, we suggest that you select the nicest hotel you can, given your curricular/itinerary needs. The cost of the hotel can be affected by the number of rooms used and length of the stay, so don't hesitate to ask the hotel for a block rate and/or length of stay discount. Outside the U.S., most hotels offer a breakfast buffet and in most it is included in the price of the room. When it is not included, there is usually a pricing option which permits you to incorporate it in the room rate. We highly recommend that you select a hotel with this option and you incorporate it into the cost for the students. Some hotels will do the same for the cost of Wi-Fi (when it is not provided for free) and given student usage of the service, we strongly suggest you include this cost as well.

As a rule of thumb, when booking our rooms, we attempt to stay under $200 per night U.S. This can be very challenging in some places and during certain seasons. If possible, we try to travel to these locations in the off-season by selecting the timing of the courses accordingly. On the other hand, in some parts of the world, the exchange rate can be so advantageous that this type of budget enables you to stay in very nice hotels. Regardless, remember the selection of the hotel should be primarily determined by the curricular and itinerary needs and only in part be determined by price (see Chapter Three for an extensive discussion of hotel selection).

We suggest that you calculate hotel costs housing two students per room and each faculty in a single room. There may be an inclination to put more than two students in each room, but this is not advisable unless you can be assured that each student will have their own full-sized bed. You do not want to be responsible for forcing students to share a bed, nor do you want to have students sleeping on the floor or child's size rollaway (which can be the alternative provided by the hotel) especially if they have paid the same price for your trip as those who get their own bed. We have colleagues who frequently travel with three or four students per room. We have observed that in these cases it is common (particularly among the men) for one or more students to feel they have to sleep on the floor rather than share a bed. This invariably leads to tension and unhappiness in the group. Faculty should have single rooms for privacy and much needed rest.

THE BUDGET

A note about hostels: Hostels can be a very inexpensive way to house your group, but we would argue against it. Youth hostels (even when they are technically "budget hotels") often place your group in the midst of many other college students who may not be traveling for academic purposes. Depending on the housing arrangements, security at hostels may not be sufficient. Additionally, the other groups staying in the hostel may serve to be a much greater distraction than would the other guests in a nice hotel, if not a poor influence on your group.

> We were once placed in a hostel in Berlin by a local agent who supposedly knew the facility well. The hostel had a patio bar in the center of the compound that remained open until 4:00 a.m., with loud music, and was frequented by many local college students. As we were visiting in summer (during a heat wave) and the hostel had no air conditioning, everyone in our group was forced to leave their windows open and were kept awake all night by the noise. In the morning the small breakfast area was swamped by the number of students trying to get their "free breakfast" and many of our students were forced to forgo their breakfast in order for us to depart on time. If such issues were to arise at even a basic hotel, appeals to the management might have yielded some satisfactory resolution but at a youth hostel such issues are more likely to be overlooked or considered the price of the bargain.

Ground Transportation

If you are going to use public transportation as your primary means of moving between locations and events, we strongly suggest that you attempt to determine how much students will need to spend on subway or bus passes. Many U.S. students have never used public transportation and they are unfamiliar with how much this may cost. We suggest you determine your public transportation needs and then choose the appropriate travel card/plan.

If you will be using public transportation extensively, you should consider purchasing an unlimited travel card (where available) for whatever period of time is appropriate. This will be the easiest way to not have to spend time at train stations reloading passes. (Trust us; you WILL spend time every day waiting for students to add funds to their subway cards if you do not purchase unlimited access). On the other hand, if you are only going to use public transportation once or twice, single use purchases may be the best option as the cost difference between single use and unlimited plans can be considerable. Also, take into consideration the zones or areas where you will be traveling most often. In cities such

THE BUDGET

as London or Paris, if you are going to go to the outer limits of the public transit, adding access to the remote locations is expensive for unlimited travel. It may be worth it to simply pay the extra fee to go to that location on a particular day.

Collecting the funds needed for ground transportation ahead of time is advisable. That way you can quickly purchase the cards upon arrival in the station the first time. Having collected all the funds ahead of time will facilitate the use of a single credit card or possibly a single transaction to purchase all of the passes. Alternatively, some train or subway stations may not have an attendant and pass purchases are limited to machines. If this is the case, it may be a bit time consuming to use a single card to make multiple purchases. If you have a particularly large group, you may want to have each student purchase their own pass using multiple machines at the same time. If you go this route, it is important to let students know that you will require them to pay for this themselves and what the approximate costs will be.

Most major cities' public transportation systems have websites, which will facilitate your determination of costs and choice of logistics. You may want to consult with a local guide or travel agent on this question as well. They may be able to purchase the passes ahead of time and definitely should be able to inform your decision.

Alternatively, you may decide to use a private coach for your transportation as we discussed in Chapter Three. If you are arranging this type of transportation yourself (as opposed to having a tour company do it), we suggest you select a transportation company that is well-known with an established safety and performance record. You and your students' safety is critical, so do your research. The most highly rated companies are also likely to be some of the more expensive providers, but depending on your itinerary, you are going to be spending a fair amount of time on the buses, and they can make a huge difference in your overall experience. You want a reliable, experienced company that will enable you to adhere to your scheduled itinerary and provide safe, comfortable transportation. Some places you may want to travel will demand specific vehicle requirements (such as traveling in the Himalayas where large buses are impractical). Therefore, the transportation company's knowledge of local transportation requirements, schedules, and rules is invaluable.

Before you select a discount provider, make sure they will be able to meet your needs in terms of things like the number and type of buses you desire (with air conditioning, for example), the qualification of drivers (licensed), or the ability of the drivers to speak English. Spending a bit more may turn out to make a big difference for your group.

If the bus is staffed by both a driver and an assistant (who may help park the bus or hand out water bottles), you will need to take into consideration the cost of tipping these people when appropriate (see the discussion later on tipping).

THE BUDGET

In many cases, we have had the experience that the same bus driver and assistant have stayed with the group over a series of days or weeks and in one case the entire trip. We recommend you build into your budget the cost of tipping as well as the provision of some small gift for these people as they play an integral role in the success of your trip.

Meals

Whether you are going to include the cost of meals in the price you charge students or not, you will need to consider the cost, location, and timing of meals in your daily planning as well as overall itinerary. As we mentioned previously, optimally, you will have selected a hotel with a breakfast option included, so that is one element of cost that you do not have to consider in your budget. For other meals, however, you will need to at least provide an estimate for students as to what they can expect to spend per day on meals as well as include the cost of **your** meals in the overall expenses on the trip.

Many institutions set limits for faculty meal reimbursements either in total or on the reimbursable amount lacking receipts. It is important that you discuss with the appropriate university administrators ahead of time any expectations they may have concerning the amount of your per diem meal reimbursement and receipt requirements. No matter what, the budgeted cost of your meals can be, at least initially, determined by your university's reimbursement policy.

Depending on your location and itinerary, you may end up eating dinner in your hotel more than you might otherwise. Hotel restaurants usually provide a variety of options that will satisfy the group but can be more expensive than outside options. Therefore, it is important to consider carefully what you may spend on meals when calculating the faculty costs.

So, what should the estimate be? Well, of course, it depends on the exchange rate and your ability to access multiple dining options, as well as how daring you are regarding your dining options. But in general, you can budget $60.00–75.00 per day in food. This is based on the assumption that you do not have to pay for breakfast. This may sound high, and in many cases, it will be much more than you end up spending, but it is always better to over-estimate your costs. If you consider the cost of eating both lunch and dinner in a hotel or other mid-range restaurant in the U.S., it is easy to imagine spending $25.00–30.00 per meal, so $60.00–75.00 per day is not unreasonable. (Just check out the prices for a club sandwich and a soda at a local hotel, and you will see how easy it is to spend $25.00 on lunch). If you are likely to be on a tight budget, it is advisable to carefully examine the historical exchange rates as well as meal price options in the different countries and cities you will visit when you create your budget.

If you are not working with a tour agent, including the cost of student meals in the overall price you charge is **not** advisable. It will be virtually impossible for you to estimate what each student might spend on meals—when you are paying—unless you can select each restaurant ahead of time and ensure they have fixed pricing, or unless, of course, you grossly overestimate the cost and intentionally collect much more than you will need. On the other hand, some tour companies can arrange for some/all of your meals to be included in the price they charge. If this is an option, it can be a tremendous benefit for your students in terms of planning. The key will be for you to consult with the tour operator on the caliber, cost, and menu options available so that you can ensure the proper fit for your students' preferences. Of course, if you have students who are unwilling to be adventurous or flexible in what/where they eat, restaurant selection can become problematic and you may want to leave selection of restaurants and paying for meals up to the students themselves.

> Once while traveling in China we had a student inform us that she "did not do vegetables" and the only meat she would eat was beef. Even a basic understanding of Chinese food should have forewarned her that this could be an issue but as she later told us she assumed "we could always go to McDonald's." This attitude was not only irritating, as you can imagine, it forced us to locate alternative dining options for many of our planned meals.

Travel and Medical Insurance

Most universities will require that you and your students purchase travel insurance as well as international medical insurance. If they do not have such a requirement, make it a requirement for your course/trip. Most U.S.-based health insurance programs will not cover expenses incurred abroad, or at best, they will only partially reimburse you for expenditures. The relatively small cost of these types of insurance is insignificant compared to the potential costs of any medical treatment, hospitalization, or trip cancellation, which can occur. Your university will likely have someone designated as responsible for purchasing both types of insurance so as a starting point, consult with this person for cost estimates. That said, the price of trip insurance is determined by the cost of the airfare and on-ground costs, as these represent the potential losses if the trip had to be canceled. You will need to have an estimate of these costs when consulting about the insurance costs. The price of the international travel insurance is also based on the coverage provided and the age of the travelers. As the costs are determined by age ranges, chances are most, if not all, of your students will fall into a single category for international travel insurance. The instructors are likely to be the only participants who fall into a separate age category and will cost slightly more. Therefore, you do not necessarily have to have the exact ages of each participant in order to determine the estimate. You must, however, determine the insurance cost per traveler so that you can include this in your course fee (if it is not simply billed to the student account). You will also want to determine if the university will pay for **your** insurance, whether that cost is billed to your department, or charged to the trip and thus passed along to the students in the course fee.

Passports and Visas

The cost of obtaining a passport can be significant depending on how quickly it is needed. We suggest that you leave the process and cost of application up to the individual student traveler (although you should expect that some students will need your assistance in filling out the application) but that you emphasize the need to get a passport from the beginning of your advertising of the study abroad experience. We regularly include the link to the U.S. State Department passport application page in all our advertising and pre-deposit communication. The passport processing time can take months; therefore, it is important that students begin the application process early. Make it clear to your students that you will not be able to purchase international airfare for the group without everyone's passport and that you will want to take advantage of early booking discounts, so they must have their passports ASAP. The timing and individual nature of the application process are such that it is usually not practical to include the passport application fee in your travel fee. (Some students already have passports; others may have issues that require a special application process, etc.).

Many of the nations you seek to visit will require a visa. You will need to research the visa requirements and application process well ahead of time. Visa requirements may differ significantly for U.S. and non-U.S. citizens, so make sure to consider the various nationalities in your group or at least the typical demographic for your university. Some nations will permit on-line visa applications, which will require the applicant to enter a credit card for payment.

Therefore, it may not be necessary to include the visa application cost in your trip fees; students can simply use their own credit or debit cards when they apply. Other nations will require you to present passports and applications at an embassy or consulate. If you are not lucky enough to live in the city where the embassy or consulate is located, additional handling fees will be involved. In major cities with embassies and consulates, there are companies that specialize in facilitating the visa application process, including the handling and delivery of the visa application and passport to the appropriate governmental officials for a flat price. We should warn you, should the visa application be returned after review or denied for any reason, they will charge an additional handling fee for reapplying. Finally, you will need to provide for the secure delivery and return of your materials to the handling agency, so you should include in your budget the additional cost of express mail delivery for each application iteration. Finally, you should speak with your university international office to see if they have a preferred visa handling agency and what those costs might be.

You will want to consider informing your students of the costs of having to re-submit a visa application as well as determine ahead of time whether you will charge students for the extra costs if their visa application is rejected or has to be redone due to their own errors. If visa applications cannot be done on-line, then we recommend that the cost of the initial application attempt be included in the course cost, but secondary attempts be treated as additional charges to students as it is unfair to drain the group's resources to pay for individual student application errors or visa denials.

> We once had to send visa applications back to the consulate five times before all our students were able to fill out the form correctly and be approved. This cost us hundreds of dollars in unplanned processing and FedEx costs. Therefore, it is vital that you ensure your students fill out the forms carefully.

You should also consider how to handle the situation of a student being permanently denied a visa. If this occurs, you will likely need to reimburse the entire cost of the trip to the student as they will not be able to travel with you. If you have already purchased airfare or made deposits for hotels, etc., this may be problematic. Make sure to discuss with your university any policies regarding reimbursement conditions and be sure to inform students (in writing) of such policies at the time of their registration.

Entrance to Sites

Many of the sites you may want to include in your itinerary will have some form of entry fee. These should be fairly easy to determine ahead of time as virtually all will have websites with all the appropriate information, or you can obtain that information from your local tour guide or travel website. Entrance fees to historical sites or museums are rarely too expensive but these costs can add up over the course of the trip, so it is important that you collect sufficient funds to cover these costs. Many of the sites will have special pricing available for groups and/or for students so you will want to take advantage of this and make sure to instruct your students to carry their university ID with them at all times. Most tour companies will include the purchasing of entrance to sites in their packages but even if they do not or you are coordinating this on your own, we highly suggest that you include the cost of all the activities in the fixed price charged to students. If the sites selected are integral to your curriculum, then each student should be required to attend and having pre-paid participation will decrease the likelihood that they will seek to skip certain activities (or at least reduce their justification for not participating).

Tips & Gratuities

Tipping etiquette varies across countries and cultures. In some places, it is expected while in others it may be considered insulting. Check travel websites or with your tour company and colleagues to determine the local etiquette and customs. Most likely, there will be a need for you to tip a variety of people. Some tour agents handling local arrangements will include the cost of tips in their fee. In that case, all the hotel staff who may handle your bags or the assistants who pre-purchase tickets for entrance to your sites, etc. will be tipped by the tour agent, saving you the trouble of determining how much to tip. This is a very nice service and if available, we recommend you take advantage of it. It can also be safer to permit the tour agent to handle tipping as the most popular tourist sites where you are likely to have to do the tipping are often plagued by pick-pockets, and you would rather not be carrying a great deal of cash.

Even with the service of your tour agent, there will undoubtedly be other tips required and for which you must account. Local tour guides and bus drivers on your private coach (even if provided by your tour agent) are classic examples. The rule of thumb here is that the longer the person worked with/for your group, the larger the tip you should expect to provide. Of course, the ease of working with your group should also be considered. If your group has made a number of unusual requests or been especially taxing (by running late or not listening), then you should perhaps tip a bit more. While we don't recommend it, if you are going to leave tipping up to your students, make sure to discuss with them the cultural expectations (such as the proper amount and who to tip) of the places you will visit. This is one area of international travel with which the students are often unfamiliar and slightly uncomfortable.

THE BUDGET

> A common and popular activity for our group is a rickshaw ride through Old Delhi. The streets of Old Delhi are so narrow that no cars are permitted, and many use two-seater rickshaws powered by a person riding a bicycle. Our students enjoy this activity, but it invariably leaves them uncertain as to the appropriate tip. Since not all the rickshaws finish the tour at the same time, in the past many of our students have felt as though they should handle the tip before the instructors could get there to give guidance. We saw some students not tip at all (assuming it was part of what the tour agent did) while others tipped extravagantly. We have learned to prepare our students beforehand on the tipping expectations of this particular activity.

Small Gifts to Distribute to Your Hosts, Assistants, and Supporters

Above and beyond a tip, it is always nice to provide a small recognition to the people who make your trip a positive experience such as the local tour guides, bus drivers, etc. This practice is extremely common outside the U.S. so don't be surprised if you are given gifts by your various hosts. You will want to be prepared to reciprocate. Even if it is not a reciprocal arrangement, we have found that gifts from America such as mugs, tee shirts, water bottles with our university logo on them are well received. Remember, you are a guest and for some of these people (who will likely never see you again) these small souvenirs are big mementos that they will appreciate and remember for years to come. You should also consider purchasing small items as thank you gifts for those back on campus who assisted in the funding or production of your course-based travel. There are likely to be numerous staff people who helped you put this all together and they will greatly appreciate some remembrance of the trip. On many campuses, the International Office (or whoever handles international guests, international students, and/or study abroad trips) will have small items with your university logo to give as gifts. Consult with them as they may be happy to provide them for you to give out as you travel.

You will undoubtedly feel the need to purchase some gifts for those back on campus, so it is best to include the funds in your budget if possible, so you do not have to pay them out of pocket. Remember, it is literally the thought that counts, so look for small mementos as you will have to carry them back with you. You can also look for "bulk" items at popular sites. Whether it is a bag of miniature Eifel Towers or boomerangs from Australia, these small souvenirs will be appreciated and don't have to cost much. To determine how much you will need for all these "small gifts," consult with your tour company ahead of time about how many

THE BUDGET

Table 5.3 Cost Planning Sheet

Costs
Airfare per person
Hotel per person
Ground transportation per person
Meals per person per day
Insurance
Visas
Entrance to sites/museums per person
Tips/gifts per person
Extras
Total cost per person[a]

[a] Note: The per person cost will not be an accurate reflection of the fee you will need to charge students. See the following discussion on What to Charge.

aids, guides, drivers, etc. you can expect to work with, and simply jot down all the people on campus who have assisted you. This should give you an estimate of the number of gifts. You can then determine how much to spend on each.

So, let's do the math on your trip. We have included a checkoff sheet to help you determine the costs for your trip (Table 5.3).

SOURCES OF FUNDING FOR THE TRIP

Financing a course-based study abroad trip most frequently boils down to the amalgamation of funds from a variety of sources. Don't be surprised or discouraged if you find yourself going hat-in-hand around campus (and off campus), raising money in $500.00 increments.

Your Students

Despite whether we like the idea, many universities pass along the costs of the faculty participation in course-based study abroad to the students who decide to participate. They simply add up the expected costs to be incurred by faculty, then distribute that across the expected number of participants, and include it in the overall price for the student. Depending on the faculty student ratio on your trip, this can significantly increase the price per student. The higher the cost of the trip, however, the fewer students who will be able to benefit from the experience. Therefore, anything you can do to find other/additional sources of support to help cover your participation is advisable.

In order to ensure that you have the funds you will need, and students have enough time to raise the money, we recommend that you develop a schedule of payments. Not all your students will need to spread out the cost of the trip over several months, but many will. We suggest that you start with a down payment that can be used as a tool to measure how many students really are serious about the class and trip. If you do not have a sufficient number of students who make the first payment by your deadline, then you know to cancel the trip. Collecting the cost of the trip over a period of several months (and yes, this may mean that students are making payments in the semester prior to travel) will ensure that you collect sufficient funds for deposits, etc., which will be required of you prior to traveling, but it will also ease the burden for the students. You should build the payment schedule around when you will need to purchase airfare and make hotel deposits, etc. If students end up having financial difficulties and cannot raise the funds needed, a payment schedule may help you discover this early in the process and not when you have already expended money on their behalf. As we mentioned previously, we also suggest that you make all payments non-refundable to ensure that student participation whims do not end up jeopardizing your finances.

The University's Contribution

The first place to start when looking for funds is with your home institution. Universities vary widely in terms of which office (or offices) bears responsibility for overseeing course-based study abroad, so you may have to spend some time initially discovering who deals with this activity. But once you have identified them, you will want to have a detailed discussion about how much financial support is available from the university.

The primary question you will have of your institution is whether they will cover the faculty costs for the trip. Some universities will pay for the travel costs of faculty leaders, others expect those costs to be passed along to the students. If the university does not have a system or policy in place to cover the faculty cost, then the per student cost will be significantly higher and your ability to recruit students will diminish. In this case, it becomes imperative that you locate as many other sources of funding as possible so that you can lower the overall cost for students.

So, Who Do I Ask?

Just because you have been given an overview of who is responsible for study abroad on your campus, don't think you cannot approach other entities on campus for support. Of course, it depends on your own campus environment, but in many cases, there are numerous offices you can ask for support.

Most universities have an international office or study abroad office. These departments may or may not be responsible for course-based study abroad activities, but it is definitely worth the time to visit with them about support. They may have direct funding or travel awards for faculty, students, or groups, or they may be aware of other sources of funding in the university or greater community.

Unlike traditional study abroad, course-based study abroad is distinctly linked to an academic offering on the main campus. Therefore, the cost of at least some part of the trip *may be* considered an expense tied to a departmental or college activity. Again, funding models vary across universities, but the argument can be made that colleges and departments must have the resources they need to deliver curriculum and the costs of instruction for these classes should include at least the faculty travel costs. Accordingly, there may be at least some support available in your department or dean's office.

You should also consider how the course-based study abroad experience is linked to your research agenda. Undoubtedly, the class you are teaching which is going to travel falls within your field of expertise, and it is your own passion and research which brought you to this point. If there is a way to incorporate your research into the travel, you may be able to request funding from the research or grants office on your campus. You might also consider incorporating student research into the course. International travel may provide a truly unique opportunity for students to conduct original research and there is growing emphasis in higher education on engaging students in research and service learning. As such, there may be funds available both on and off your campus to help fund such activities. Speak with your Dean and/or office of research for suggestions for support.

Globalization and internationalizing the curriculum have become a key objective in many of our institutions. If that is the case on your campus, then take advantage of it. If it is a strategic priority of your university, then consider approaching the provost, president, and/or chancellor's office for support, if that would be considered acceptable on your campus. While there is widespread acceptance of the educational value of an international experience, few of our institutions can fund these activities to the point of meeting all the needs. So, your solicitation for funding will mostly likely not be a total surprise to any of the university officials you approach. Once again, contributions of small amounts from numerous offices can go a long way to covering faculty costs, lowering student costs, and facilitating participation. Such requests may also help increase the saliency of the funding question for all international experiences, so it cannot hurt to ask.

We suggest you also consider external funding sources such as www.gooverseas.com/blog/study-abroad-scholarships-grants Rotary Clubs (www.rotary.org/en/our-programs/scholarships), the consulate of the country you will be traveling to, the Global Access Pipeline (https://globalaccesspipeline.org/), and fraternal orders such as the Elks (www.elks.org/) and the Moose Lodge, as these organizations sometimes have funds available for international travel which may assist you in developing and funding course-based study abroad. There is also country specific funding for some locations. For example, if you plan on going to Germany, the Marshall Fund provides support for students to study there. Some of these sources fund university level initiatives to develop or enhance the infrastructure to support study abroad, while others subsidize individual courses/excursions. They often have a regional preference or seek to support certain types of co-curricular activities, such as service learning. Nevertheless, a search of these programs can be useful for funding as well as insights into the places and activities others have used to enhance the travel experience. Most of these grants are going to require significant lead-time between application and travel, so you should begin your exploration as soon as possible.

HOW MUCH DO I CHARGE?

Per Student Costs

Once you have determined the total costs and the sources of support that may be available for your trip, you will need to determine the cost per student. The number of students you are willing to take with you should be determined by the number of faculty participating and other travel logistics (see Chapter Six for a detailed discussion). That said, in our experience, the number of students on your trip is rarely determined by faculty preferences of group size. Student recruitment is much more likely to be determined by the overall cost of the trip. You should determine the **minimum** number of students needed and set your course fee based on that. If you are lucky enough to attract more students than you expected and in doing so you end up collecting "extra" money, it can always be returned to the students. Having these supplemental funds available on the trip in case of emergency (or excess baggage fees) is advisable. Student accounts can be refunded upon your return.

To determine cost, simply create a list of all the estimated costs. You will want to start by determining the cost for faculty and then calculate the costs for students. You need to calculate these separately: Faculty costs will be higher than student

THE BUDGET

costs, given that faculty should be using single hotel rooms and have all meals covered, and may need to have some amount of additional funds for emergencies.

Take a look at the following example, taken from a recent course-based study abroad experience, which involved traveling to India for three plus weeks (27 days). This example is based on the assumption that the student course fee was to be used to cover the expenses of two faculty members and that a minimum of 15 students would participate (Tables 5.4 and 5.5).

Table 5.4 Sample Faculty Cost

Costs (per faculty member)	
Airfare (estimate)	$2000.00
Hotel & Tour package (includes single occupancy hotel, all in country ground transportation and entrance to all sites/museums	$4095.00
Meals (based on $40 per day—University allowance)	$1080.00
Visas	$60.00
Tips, etc.	$100.00
Total cost 1 faculty	**$7335.00**
Total cost 2 faculty	**$14,670.00**
Subtotal	**$14,670.00**
Departmental support	$1500.00
Dean support	$3000.00
Total cost of the faculty portion	**$10,170.00**

Table 5.5 Sample Student Cost Course Fee

Costs (per student)	
Airfare	$2,000.00
Hotel & tour package (includes double occupancy hotel, all in country ground transportation and entrance to sites/museums)	$3,015.00
Meals (breakfast included in hotel—no other meals included)	$0.00
Visas	$60.00
Tips, etc.	$50.00
Faculty cost (2 faculty divided by 15 students)	$678.00
Total	**$5,803.00**

So, the course fee charged to students would be $5,803.00. For comfort sake, we would suggest you simply round that figure up to $5,900.00 or $6,000.00.

It is important that you build in a bit of a buffer. No matter how accurately you may have budgeted, it is highly likely that there will be incidentals either for the group or just the faculty which were not accounted for. It could be something as simple as having to have your laundry done in the hotel (which can be costly) or having to pay for alternative transportation for the group when a bus or train is missed. No matter what, it is better to collect a little extra as a contingency. We usually recommend $100.00–$200.00 per student, depending on the length of the trip.

> We once had our bus break down in the height of Delhi traffic. Neither tow trucks nor alternative buses could get through the traffic jam to address our situation. Eventually, we had to hire a series of auto rickshaws (which hold only three people each) to take the entire group to our next stop as it was the last before we headed to the airport for the flight home. It was not only comical to see 10 or so auto rickshaws weaving in and out of traffic, it was an unexpected transportation cost.

THE STUDENT BUDGET

The course fee should cover the majority of the cost of the trip for your students, but it does not represent 100% of what they will need. Students will have to have additional funds available to cover anything not included in your fee as well as their own shopping/spending preferences.

The more of the costs of the trip that you can include in the overall price, the less uncertainty there will be for your students in planning for their financial needs. Students are often completely unprepared to correctly estimate how much money they will need for international travel and they frequently find the prospect overwhelming. It is rare that students over-estimate their costs and have MORE money than they need while traveling. Therefore, it is critical that you be able to assist the students in their calculations. If they do not have the money they need to do all the things they want to do, students are guaranteed to be unhappy. More importantly, they may run out of funds to do the things required of the itinerary and/or begin to skimp on meals, which will eventually make them nervous and irritable, and generally ruin the travel experience. In the end, you may end up covering some of the student costs if they run out of money, so it is important to help them budget correctly.

THE BUDGET

On most trips, our students are responsible for the cost of all or most of their meals. Unfamiliarity with exchange rates and the cost of eating in hotel restaurants may lead students to underestimate the cost of their meals. It is important that you point out to students that the amount they use at home to determine their food budget is not sufficient. That calculation will not take into account eating **all** meals and snacks out (something they rarely do at home) and while traveling they may not always have the option of choosing the restaurant (and in doing so picking a less expensive option). As the group moves through the itinerary, there are likely to be times where you will have to grab meals or snacks when they are available/convenient. Finding a restaurant that can seat your entire group and has a fairly diverse menu to please as many as possible often means that cost becomes the less important criteria. Students need to recognize this and plan accordingly. You can use the same daily meal estimate for students as you would for yourself (if you were not constricted by your university reimbursement policy): $60.00–75.00 per day (not including breakfast). Of course, this amount may vary by country and exchange rate, but it is important that students do not underestimate these costs.

> We once had a student with us in Germany for a month who budgeted so poorly (despite our best efforts to prepare her) that she believed she would be happy with only one meal a day. As you can imagine, this not only made her unhappy but also eventually caused issues with the group when others bought her meals, feeling sorry for her, only to see her spend money on alcohol.

Airline baggage fees are additional costs which students never seem to plan for. If nothing else, students will likely have to plan on spending $50.00–100.00 to check their bags to/from the country of your experience. If you plan on having students contribute to cover the excess baggage fees as they occur, you need to provide students an estimate for that cost.

If your students are primarily from a part of the country where there is little public transportation, it is going to be important to help them calculate how much they are going to need for subway passes or other public transportation if these are not completely included in your costs. In a new city, students will be unsure of the distances they will want to cover and how that may affect the costs of transportation. So, you will need to develop an estimate for these.

If there is one aspect of study abroad about which we are most confident, it is that students are going to spend a lot on souvenirs and keepsakes. You can help students determine how much they might need by discussing ahead of time the type of handicrafts and/or experiences they might be interested in purchasing while traveling. If you know the itinerary has time set aside for students to take advantage of particular activities such as traveling to nearby cities over an off weekend, taking surfing lessons, attending a Broadway show, or touring museums which were not included in the class activities fee, then you will want to discuss this with the students ahead of time. Give them an idea of what they may be interested in purchasing or doing and how much it costs. They love to shop so expect that they will be doing that everywhere they go. Helping them plan accordingly can go a long way to avoiding the unhappiness of students running out of money.

With all the costs to be borne by the students, it is critically important that you discuss and help students plan for fluctuations in the exchange rate. Using the historical strength of the U.S. dollar against the local currency, you should be able to give the students a sense of how far their money will go while traveling. We recommend a class or pre-departure activity where students track some of their common daily expenditures, look up what these items cost abroad and then using the monthly average exchange rate, calculate how much (in U.S. dollars) they would need to make these purchases. Additionally, if there are certain items that you know your students may want but perhaps are priced differently aboard (such as Wi-Fi access—which they expect to be free—or Starbucks coffee), you might want to have the students repeat the exercise using these items.

As you move through the exercises to estimate costs with the students you can provide them this simple budget sheet so that they can truly envision the cost of the trip (Table 5.6).

Table 5.6 Student Budget—Outside the Course Fee

Costs
Meals
Souvenirs
Baggage fees
Extra transportation costs
Total

SOURCES OF FUNDING FOR STUDENTS

Clearly, you cannot be responsible for the student costs of course-based study abroad. But you should expect many students to find the cost of the trip intimidating and so the more ideas you have to share with students about where they might seek funding, the better.

An important source of student funding for study abroad is scholarships and grants. The first thing we tell every student who expresses any interest in any of our trips is: Go Talk To The Financial Aid Office! There are a number of national and international scholarships that are specifically for study abroad which can be quite beneficial. Most of these will require significant lead-time, so the sooner your students know about your trip and begin to apply for funding the better. These funding sources will differ in the destinations they prefer, the length of travel they will cover, and the academic requirements. Whether the proposed study abroad experience is required for a student's degree can also be a key aspect of whether funding is available. You may want to provide your university's financial aid office a thorough description of your course and trip, so they can best identify the funding sources that might be most appropriate.

We also suggest that you discuss with the financial aid office whether there are any on-campus scholarships which might be available. Many universities have grants for study abroad housed either in the financial aid or in the international programs office. Some universities may consider study abroad as similar to the educational benefits as research presentations and conference travel, so it is possible that students could apply for funding with your university's research office or other relevant office. Students should also inquire with their college and academic departments whether any funding is available. While usually not large amounts, many colleges and departments have some amount of discretionary funding available for student travel for academic purposes. Even a small grant of a couple of hundred dollars can be significant in helping a student have the money they need, so it is worth a thorough search.

Over the years, we have watched our students get very creative in their efforts to raise funds for study abroad. One common strategy, which we now recommend, is for students to tell all their family and friends that this experience is something important to them and ask for donations. Given the 7- to 10-month lead-time between signing up and actually traveling, students can request financial donations in lieu of birthday, Christmas, and other holiday gifts. We have observed relatives are particularly supportive of this activity when students show their commitment to this educational experience by forfeiting other gifts. Even their friends and contemporaries can help. If they ask each of 10 friends to donate $10.00 instead of giving a gift on special occasions, students will have $100.00 to spend on the trip (and their friends get an inexpensive gift option!).

In a couple of cases, our classes or individual students have hosted fundraisers to offset the cost of travel. These can be done on campus or off and can take any number of forms (from class popcorn sales to babysitting services for faculty with children), but the key seems to be the advertisement of **why** students are fundraising. Just as the case with family members, telling people they are raising funds for a course they are taking which will travel seems to make a favorable impression and yield donations. The appropriateness of this as organized activities of your class must be determined in light of the expectations and culture of your campus, but there is nothing to stop individual students from adapting this idea to their own fundraising.

CONCLUSION

Every trip, every student, and every university is different, so this chapter provides guidelines rather than hard and fast rules. Even the most carefully planned budget can result in a shortfall for myriad reasons. Something as simple as the dollar becoming weaker than expected against the currency of the country you are traveling to can throw off a budget. Inflation, currency devaluation, and even your guarantees of certain amenities or services as included that then turn out to be available only for an extra fee can increase the costs of your trip and burn through your budget faster than you planned. Have your budget as well as a bit extra for the unexpected.

CHECKLIST

Costs

- ☐ Use of a tour company
- ☐ Airline costs
- ☐ Excess baggage
- ☐ Hotel accommodations
- ☐ Ground transportation
- ☐ Meals
- ☐ Travel and medical insurance
- ☐ Passports and visas
- ☐ Entrance to sites
- ☐ Tips & gratuities

THE BUDGET

Sources of Funding for the Trip
- [ ] Your students
- [ ] The university's contribution
- [ ] So, who do I ask?

How Much Do I Charge?
- [ ] Per student costs
- [ ] The student budget
- [ ] Sources of funding for students

Chapter Six

Responsibility

Course-based study abroad often takes faculty to new places within their own university as well as around the world. Coordinating a study abroad experience will most likely introduce you to people and offices across campus that ordinarily you would have little cause to visit. While the University bears responsibility for virtually all administrative, legal, financial, management, and logistical aspects of these endeavors, quite frequently they lack a streamlined process for handling course-based travel. Therefore, you should expect to have to oversee the entirety of the process so that you can be assured everything goes as planned.

Faculty should take the time to thoroughly discuss all aspects of the trip with the appropriate university administrators (such as your department chair, dean, and the director of the study abroad office) so that you know precisely what type of expectations there are, what kind of support is available, and where responsibility lies. These things range from questions concerning the logistics or planning of the trip to liability in the case something goes wrong. These topics can be categorized as logistics, trip management, financial, professional, and liability questions. You need to clarify what the roles and responsibilities of the institution are and what are left to you.

It is important to note that the discussion that follows is based on the optimal balance of institutional and faculty responsibilities. In many institutions, the support and expertise described later may not exist and faculty will be left to coordinate the various aspects of course-based study abroad. Nevertheless, here we present what we believe is the appropriate distribution of responsibility. If in discussions on your own campus you discover that there is not the level of institutional support discussed later, you may want to consider how much of this responsibility you are willing to take on yourself.

UNIVERSITY RESPONSIBILITY

Logistics

The first thing you will want to investigate on your campus is who and which office is responsible for course-based study abroad experiences. Most universities have a study abroad office, but that does not necessarily mean that they will oversee or support on-ground courses that include a travel component. So, you will need to determine if these activities fall under your academic unit or some other part of the university, or if they are shared responsibilities. As a starting point, we suggest that you meet with other faculty who have led course-based study abroad on your campus. They will have insights and advice on how to maneuver through the university bureaucracy that may prove to be invaluable. It is the university's job to handle the various aspects of study abroad, but don't be surprised if you have to determine who on your campus actually does the work of the planning and coordinating the trip.

When you meet with each appropriate university official, you need to ask about a variety of things concerning setting up your trip. You should start with a discussion of what the approval process may be to determine whether faculty are permitted to lead study abroad trips. Universities with a long history of faculty-student travel will undoubtedly have a mechanism in place to provide formal approval of your participation and the specific trip. If your university does not, we suggest that you at least solicit a letter from your dean (or higher administrator) indicating the university has officially approved of you and any other faculty participants leading a trip. This formal statement will serve as documentation of the university's endorsement of the trip and your ability to lead it—if that should ever prove necessary. If nothing else, your request may begin a much-needed discussion on your campus of who is eligible to lead these trips.

The university should be able to tell you whether you are permitted to use pre-packaged tours or develop your own itinerary. Some universities discourage the use of pre-packaged tours while others are ambivalent. The university should also be able to give you information on tour operators they have used in the past and hopefully some evaluations of those. No matter which you use, you will want to inquire about the procedures to create a study abroad class, and how that will be billed/paid for. The university should be prepared to have the travel cost attached to the course as a course fee, as well as handle any registration requirements. Having the cost of travel added to the class as a course fee can increase the possibility of a student's financial aid covering at least some part of the travel, so if you can set it up this way it will increase the number of students who can afford to participate. To accomplish this, you will likely need to speak to not only the registrar (who controls the course registration process) but also whomever in your area creates the course schedule. They need to include notations in the schedule indicating that this class entails course-based study abroad **and** that there is a course fee. If that is not apparent to students when they are registering for classes, it is likely that you will have people accidentally register for your class who are not aware of the cost and time implications of your travel. We also suggest that you set up the course so that registration requires the instructor's signature, to ensure that the only people registering for your class are those you have approved and have made their deposits.

As we mentioned previously, it may be possible to simply offer an existing course, which for the given semester has a travel component, or to teach your class as selected topics or an independent study course, with a specialized focus on your travel area. It is not unusual for either of these types of courses to require approval (from a department chair or dean) prior to being offered, so you will want to explore your options for course offerings. While all of these considerations are clearly administrative decisions over which faculty often have little say, you should be prepared to ask before you begin advertising your class.

Once you have been approved to lead the class, you should inquire as to the procedures the institution requires for making all the travel arrangements and payments as well as how the students will make payments for the trip. In many universities much, if not all, of this work will be done for you but you will need to be familiar with them nonetheless as students and vendors alike will approach you with questions concerning costs and payments. Other universities may ask you to coordinate all this on your own. Regardless, you should inquire about who is responsible for what and your institution should be prepared to provide a detailed response such that all responsibilities are clear.

Institutional financial procedures for course-based study abroad can be cumbersome and often overwhelming for the first-time instructor. You may need to create a specific account for the trip finances, rather than simply utilizing your existing departmental accounts. Speak to your chair, dean, or the university comptroller's office to determine whether that is needed and how to go about doing so. The university must be responsible for billing for the trip as well as collecting the funds from students. You should insist that the cost of the trip be included on the students' bill or account. You do not want to be responsible for collecting the money or for having to deposit trip funds into your departmental accounts. Your university comptroller (or equivalent) should be able to create a designated account for the trip, so the funds are specifically earmarked for your trip.

Many universities have designated travel agents who can be a tremendous asset. If your university requires (or even recommends) the use of a specific person, reach out to them as soon as possible to discuss your class and travel ideas. Travel agents often have insights into aspects of international travel, which you have not begun to contemplate. Our travel agent Gail has often provided guidance on various aspects of our itinerary based on her experience with different airlines, airports, security issues, etc. which has made our work significantly easier.

It is likely that your institution will have a requirement that each traveler has international medical insurance as well as trip insurance. If they do not have such a requirement, you should make it a course requirement for your own protection and peace of mind. The university should be able to assist you in finding providers, purchasing the policies, and billing student accounts. We highly recommend you require it for your group. Such insurance is critical and can be a financial lifesaver (see the Budget chapter for insights into calculating the cost of insurance).

> On one trip we had to take seven students to the doctor in Germany for strep throat and the instructor ended up seeing a specialist three times. Our U.S.-based health insurance would have covered none of those medical costs.
>
> A volcanic eruption in Iceland in 2010 caused weather issues across Europe which resulted in major travel disruptions for weeks (see BBC 2010; Harris 2010). Several of our colleagues had trips planned during this period which had to be canceled. Having trip insurance at least provided coverage for all the cancellation costs.

The university should provide insurance for the instructors. Remember, this is an academic experience that you are leading on behalf of the university, so they are obligated to ensure that you have the appropriate coverage for any medical needs you may have on the trip as well as possible cancellation fees you may incur if you have to cancel the trip.

Composition of the Travel Group

The right combination of students (and faculty) participating in your course-based study abroad experience is critical. When you get a "good group," the travel can be easy and the teaching and learning joyful. On the other hand, the wrong combination of personalities can undermine the entire experience. Putting together a group of faculty and students who are open to and excited about the travel and the course is not an accident. There are numerous things you can do to ensure that everyone knows what to expect and that you are familiar with all the personalities you are traveling with. We discuss this in much more detail later in this chapter, but some of your efforts will be affected by university policies, so you should do some inquireis beforehand.

The university should have in place expectations for determining the appropriate student/faculty ratio and the group size. Institutional policies vary on the appropriate number of faculty needed per student and the literature in the field places the determination of the appropriate ratio squarely on the individual institutions.[1] You should find out what your university's expectations are on the student/faculty ratio and plan accordingly. We suggest no more than 8:1 and the larger the overall group, the smaller the optimal ratio. We derive this number by considering the policies of numerous other institutions. See, for example: www.depts.ttu.edu/international/studyabroad/facultypartners/faculty/Pictures_uploads/OP%2034.26%20Faculty%20Handbook-Updated%2012.2017.pdf, www.unf.edu/uploadedFiles/sa/intlctr/Faculty_Manual_for_Study_Abroad.pdf, www.savannahstate.edu/academic-affairs/docs/IEC_Procedure_Manual.pdf, https://asufdhandbook.wordpress.com/contact/). An 8:1 ratio may seem low in comparison to what you are used to in your traditional classes, but when you are attempting to keep track of everyone as they are claiming their luggage, running off to the currency exchange, or simply disappearing to go to the restroom when you arrive after a long flight, you may feel eight is quite a challenge.

It is common for Universities to require a minimum number of students participating in course-based study abroad. This may be tied to the institutional funding of your travel or it may be an artifact of the minimum class size requirement. You will want to ask what that expectation is and what will happen if you do not reach that minimum. Remember, you will likely have been developing the itinerary, working with vendors, and advertising your class as well as collecting deposits from students long before course registration occurs. The university should have considered all this and developed a mechanism to approve small classes or reimburse you for the time and effort if the class does not make because only five or six students signed up. Even if your university has no constraints on the size of your overall group, we would recommend against letting the group grow too large. The larger the group the more difficult it will be to handle all of the logistics of moving from place to place, the greater number of possible issues that can arise, and the harder it will be to create a cohesive collaborative engaged group. We strongly suggest you do not let the group grow beyond 30 students in order to facilitate the personal attention and positive group dynamics required of a study abroad experience. If you have ever had to change an assignment or escort a class to the library or outside for a fire drill, then you have experienced some of the challenges of communicating and coordinating the activities of the "adults" in your classes. Now imagine if you were trying to get a group of 40 or so students on and off the subway during rush hour.

The university should be prepared to provide you additional faculty chaperones if the group becomes too large. Attempting to stay within recommended student/faculty ratios would mean that even a group of 30 (which would not seem large for a traditional on-ground class) would require at least three faculty. If you have concerns about finding a sufficient number of faculty to participate, we suggest you inquire whether other university staff or administrators might be appropriate to chaperone. We have traveled with the Dean of Students as well as staff from the International Affairs Office as group leaders and both proved to be incredibly valuable assets to our overall experience.

The gender makeup of the faculty on the trip is also something the university should have considered and planned for. We strongly recommend you travel with at least one male and one female faculty leader. Faculty gender can be an important factor in dealing with any student issues, which may arise. In our experience, students have varying levels of comfort discussing problems or issues with members of the opposite sex and the last thing you want to happen is for a student to fail to tell you about a problem they are having which may affect the group, simply because they would prefer to speak with a man/woman.

Virtually all institutions will have policies in place concerning whether students on various forms of academic or behavioral probation can participate in study abroad or represent the university in this fashion. How strictly this is enforced or whether this can be appealed by the student is a more delicate question. You will want to make sure you are clear on whether you have the final say on questions of participation, so you should ask about the process for determining which students can travel with you.

> We once had a student insist on participating in a six-week study-abroad course. The student had a history of disciplinary issues (involving violence and drug usage) in multiple classes, on his athletic team, and in his dorm. At the time of the trip preparation, he was not on probationary status as he had been expelled from the dorm and removed from the team. He applied to participate, and when denied by the study abroad office as well as the student activities office, he appealed to the Dean and Provost. It took the insistence of all three faculty (one of whom was the student's academic advisor) that they had grave concerns about traveling with this student to ensure the thorough discussion of the requirements of participation as the institution had not faced such a situation before.

Faculty can do quite a bit to influence aspects of the travel group's composition through the structure of their course. Using pre-requisites and/or limiting the course to majors may be sufficient to ensure the students are academically prepared for the experience. Making your course a junior or senior level course may go a long way to ensuring the students who enroll are mature enough for the experience. But academic preparation and maturity may not be the only concerns. Just as you have seen in your classrooms, not all personalities add benefit to a group. Imagine the most problematic or disruptive student you have encountered. Would you want to spend 10 plus hours on a plane with them or keep track of them in a crowded subway? We suggest you make clear to all interested students that in order to participate in the trip they will be expected to be on their best behavior as well as have to take several academically demanding courses—including the coursework on the trip. The amount of work they have to do ahead of time (as well as while traveling) tends to deter students who are less vested in the trip and therefore likely to be more problematic.

We have learned over the years that the mental and physical health of your students (and faculty leaders) can have a significant effect on your travel experience. Don't assume that simply because they all appear healthy, that there will not be any issues. We have had students neglect to tell anyone they had heart issues and could not walk long distances as well as students with significant mental illness, which in one case significantly disrupted the trip. We even had one student who became pregnant prior to the trip and was plagued with morning sickness throughout the trip. If possible, you should know about these issues ahead of time, so you can work with the students to ensure that your program is the right fit for them, and so you can be prepared to make appropriate adaptations for them or deal with any problems that may arise. However, collection of information on someone's health raises a number of legal and ethical questions.

The university should have policies in place to screen students to ensure that they are healthy enough to participate and to provide faculty with the information and support needed to accommodate student needs. Faculty should not be tasked with the collection of student health information, nor is it appropriate. One way to deal with the need to know about student health concerns while maintaining privacy is to provide students with an accurate picture of the physical or psychological demands of the trip in the advertising and recruiting period prior to registration or travel. Many students may not realize the amount of walking entailed in sightseeing, the emotional nature of visiting certain locations (i.e., concentration camps), or even the exhausting nature of international travel. A thorough explanation of the itinerary and its physical/emotional demands hopefully will lead prospective students to discuss any issues or concerns they may have with you prior to traveling and thus help prevent problems which could affect their ability to participate fully.

Finally, in our experience it is not uncommon for people not associated with the university to want to participate in our study abroad experience. We have had former students as well as parents accompany us. How to accommodate or whether to permit such participants should be clear in the university's policies. As these individuals are not subject to institutional disciplinary rules, there may be questions concerning behavioral expectations and how to deal with them. Even if the university permits outside participants, faculty should still have the final say as to who accompanies the group and under what conditions. Such participants may be desirable as they may enrich the nature of the group and can help meet the minimum number needed for the trip to make and/or decrease the cost per participant, but you will want to make sure they do not undermine the academic purpose. We suggest you be explicit with those interested that academic discussion will dominate the travel and they will be expected to participate (and hopefully have done the reading).

Administrative Support

Probably the most important institutional responsibility (from the perspective of these faculty members) is the administrative support provided for all aspects of the trip. Course-based study abroad can be, as I am sure you are beginning to see, overwhelmingly time consuming. Faculty should be able to rely on various parts of the university such as the study abroad office and the comptroller's office to assist in the planning and administration of this endeavor. Institutional support for the preparation of the travel component of the class is vital not only to the production of a given course-based study abroad experience, but to the continuation of these opportunities over time. Determining the logistics of the itinerary, selecting hotels and transportation providers, as well as the visa application process are all aspects where a professional study abroad office should be able to assist. Administrative support should also be available for the publicizing of your trip, the collection of money, paying of deposits, etc.

Another critical aspect of institutional support is that of having a university official on call throughout the trip. Issues or emergencies can arise which may require assistance from those on campus. It might be something small such as needing assistance with communication with the insurance provider (which is likely based in the U.S. and could be in radically different time zones making it difficult to contact while maintaining the itinerary) or it could be something as significant as needing to remove one of the students from the trip. The university should designate an emergency contact on campus (available 24 hours a day) and make clear what services they are prepared to provide. Optimally, there should be someone on campus prepared to join the group on short notice should additional chaperones be needed, or the faculty member be unable to continue traveling or has to leave the group due to a personal emergency.

Unfortunately, universities will also need policies in place concerning whether or under what conditions faculty have the authority to send a student home (due to illness or behavioral issues for example) at some point during the travel if the need arises. Whose authorization is needed, the process for contacting this individual, and how the cost associated with these changes in travel plans would be handled, all must be made clear to both faculty and travel participants. The possibility of being prohibited from traveling or being sent home can be a key factor in student compliance with behavioral and academic expectations.

Cases such as that of Natalee Holloway[2] act as a cautionary tale for institutions and faculty alike. Traveling with students and the accidents or incidents which may arise can raise significant liability questions. The university (and faculty union, if applicable) should make clear the legal protections provided to faculty traveling with students. It should be clear whether additional designated insurance is provided for those leading course-based study abroad or whether these activities simply fall under the designation of basic responsibilities and thus would be covered under existing university policies. It should also be clear what types of issues or accidents are covered (or not) by your trip insurance.

Costs and Payment While Traveling

Even though we would encourage you to never consider leading students on international travel as a vacation, you should recognize that you will encounter costs while traveling just like you would on a personal adventure. If you do not already have one, you will have to get a passport, which (depending on when you apply) can be somewhat costly. Currently, the price for applying for a U.S. passport starts at $145.00. If you require expedited or other special services, there may be significant additional fees (https://travel.state.gov/content/travel/en/passports.html). Then, there will likely be visa application costs as well as other costs, such as international phone charges. Unless the university has an international cell phone for you to use, or you plan on purchasing a disposable phone for use while on the trip, you will have to activate your personal cell phone for international coverage, provide the number to students and parents, and keep it on in case of emergencies. Doing so will likely mean that you will incur significant fees for data, roaming, and calls. The university should be prepared to reimburse you the cost for the phone usage and visa applications at minimum as these are costs only incurred due to your participation in the class. University policies differ on the coverage of the passport application or renewal fee, so you should check to see if this is something you are going to have to pay out of pocket. Institutions that do not cover these costs should provide documentation for faculty indicating that this is an unreimbursed professional expense.

While traveling, you will need to have access to the funds you have collected for your trip. You should inquire about how that is handled on your campus. Experience would suggest that we warn you against using pre-loaded debit cards which may be provided by your institution. The international nature of your expenditures will often cause a hold to be placed on the card once it is used, making the remaining funds inaccessible for at least some amount of time. University issued credit cards will be of some value but will require a significant credit limit to cover any unexpected expenditures (we had one case where we had to use a credit card to cover the cost of admitting a student to the hospital) as well as notification to the issuing bank of all the cities to be visited and types of activities to be purchased to ensure that no holds are placed on the card for being abroad or for foreign transaction fees/delays. Additionally, credit cards are not accepted everywhere (especially in less developed areas) and travelers checks have virtually disappeared as an option, so it is likely you will need to take cash. We highly recommend that you pre-pay as much of the trip expenses as possible such as hotel and transportation costs. But even doing so, you are likely to end up with a significant amount of cash to cover all the remaining costs. Universities should be prepared to provide significant cash advances for this type of travel and we recommend that you distribute the cash across the faculty participants for security reasons and keep as much of it as is appropriate in your hotel safe whenever possible.

Teaching and Workload Considerations

Given the time and effort required to prepare and lead course-based study abroad, the value the university places on such activities should be transparent. How course-based study abroad activities fit into your academic load as well as tenure performance evaluation should be laid out in the faculty handbook. If it is not, we recommend faculty obtain a letter or other formal documentation from their dean indicating the importance of and support for course-based study abroad activities. Particularly for non-tenured faculty, this type of clarity and documentation may be critical.

Depending on the value placed on international travel and the globalization of the curriculum, there may be supplemental pay or a stipend offered to encourage these activities. On the other hand, some campuses treat these classes as being no different from traditional on-ground classes, despite the significant amount of extra work they require. Accordingly, it is important that you gain an unfiltered clarity on the question of how this work will be recognized and accounted for in your annual evaluation or tenure/promotion efforts. If the university does not provide a course release; extra pay; or some other recognition of the time, effort, and significance of course-based study abroad, we would suggest that you think carefully before agreeing to participate. If there is not recognition in the evaluation process of how such courses are significantly different from traditional classes, we cannot recommend you spend your time doing them—at least until you have earned tenure and promotion.

FACULTY RESPONSIBILITY

A good portion of what it takes to make a good international experience lies within your sphere of influence. You can make this great! But to do so, you should be clear about your responsibilities.

Coordinating the "Stuff"

In several other chapters we have detailed the importance and logistics of planning the itinerary, but it remains important to note that the overall quality of the learning experience is your responsibility. The travel should be supported by the curriculum, balancing discipline-specific knowledge to be mastered with the value of intercultural skills to be gained through travel. That's just a nice way of saying your students should find the experience both fun and educational!

Remember, you are the person that the students, their parents, and the university administration will look to in order to make sure the entirety of the course-based study abroad experience goes smoothly. One critical aspect of a positive student experience is how well the administrative aspects of the class go. You may have a significant amount of support from various offices on campus, but it is still your responsibility to ensure things run smoothly. Whether it be registration issues, student deposits and financial balance questions, or visa application challenges, it is up to the faculty to help guide students and make sure such administrative obstacles do not interfere with educational opportunities. This means you should be in close contact with various offices and staff across campus so that they can quickly and efficiently assist with any student challenges. As we mentioned earlier, take some time to get to know the individuals on your campus who will be handling the various aspects of your trip; they are critical to the success of your endeavor.

Faculty should also be prepared for the (often-challenging) task of keeping the travel and international experience positive and on track. Students can easily be disappointed or become overwhelmed when faced with challenges such as missed connections or disappointing hotel/restaurant experiences. It is up to you as the faculty leader to prevent as many of these possibilities as possible and to help students adapt if the issues arise.

Your ability to maintain positive group energy and roll with the punches can often be affected by the nature and composition of your travel class, so let's consider who should travel.

Make Sure You Are Traveling with the Right People

Carefully consider the other faculty or leaders who accompany you on the study abroad trip. You should get to know your colleagues **well** before you agree to travel with them. Traveling with students is often exhausting and difficult. You will want to have a good sense of how your colleagues handle those conditions. The best faculty leaders are flexible, good-natured, disciplined, mature, responsible, and able to think on their feet. Those with significant international travel experience of their own will have demonstrated their ability to handle the challenges that can occur. You should look for faculty who are comfortable enough with international travel that they can reassure students who may never have left the country before. Excellent classroom management skills also translate well to the demands of traveling internationally with a group, as being just a little late may mean you miss a flight or a critical destination on your itinerary.

You do not want to travel with someone who hesitates to create boundaries for the students: that can lead to all kinds of issues. Rather you want to travel with faculty who get along well with their students but have no trouble being disciplinarians if needed. Don't expect the faculty member who is known for always accepting late papers, not caring if students arrive late to class or play their phones instead of taking notes to be one to help you keep your students compliant with your travel expectations. Quite frankly, if the students take the faculty seriously before the trip even starts, they are less likely to break rules and cause trouble while traveling. On every trip, there are hiccups or unexpected developments that can present challenges. Whether that is a plane delay, a lost hotel reservation, or lost luggage, you want to be traveling with colleagues who are decisive and responsible so as to minimize the impact of these issues. Finally, you want to ensure that you have complementary teaching styles and expectations—long before you decide to travel with someone. Sending a clear message to the students about what you expect of them both academically and behaviorally is important and that will be much easier to do if all the faculty participants are in agreement.

The right combination of students is also important for a successful trip. You can help insure this by setting the academic and behavioral expectations beforehand. Give some thought to how you would like your students to approach the class as well as the travel. Be aware of your own sensitivities, for unlike a 75-minute class, you are not going to be able to escape student behavior you find irritating while traveling. If you know that never being late is important to your

RESPONSIBILITY

itinerary and an aspect of your own personal behavior, simply tell interested students that. If they understand that being late could jeopardize the itinerary and it is something you consider rude, disrespectful, and won't tolerate, they will know what to expect and hopefully make choices accordingly.

You cannot prevent all undesirable student behavior, but you can go a long way to preventing it by making it very clear to all students what your expectations are. We have found that students will often self-select not to join a course-based study abroad class if their hopes for a vacation seemed to clash with our expectation of serious academic study. Explaining to students that this is a class first, a travel experience second, is key. Emphasize in your pre-registration conversations or recruitment/information sessions the academic focus, requirements, and expectations of your trip. Some students will be looking for an opportunity to travel just to party. You want to send a message that if that is what they are looking for, your trip is not for them. If you do not dispel that expectation on the part of students before you leave the country, it will be very difficult to deal with them while traveling.

Finally, we recommend that you set the appropriate tone early on in your dealings with students. From the beginning of the class, you want students to be taking the class and their studies seriously. That means that they are doing the readings and assignments in a timely manner, engaging with the material, and generally earning the privilege of traveling with you. Students who have taken the preparatory class seriously will have a greater appreciation for the places you will travel to and have a more meaningful experience. Therefore, you need to help ensure their preparedness. You may want to be stricter with this class at the beginning of the semester than you are in your other classes. You can always ease up or become more easy-going once you are traveling, but it is virtually impossible to instill discipline once you have created a dynamic where it is not expected.

Understand the Time Requirements

Without exception, the number one observation made by first time faculty study-abroad leaders is the tremendous amount of time it takes. The time spent making preparations for the class, the time spent with students while traveling, and the time spent tying things up when you return are all going to be more than you might expect.

We provide a timeline for preparing and implementing a course-based study abroad experience in Chapter Three, but in short, you should expect to spend about a year working on such an endeavor, and that does not mean just a few hours a week. In many parts of the process, you will find that you need to devote most of your day/week to these activities. If leading course-based study abroad activities is not significantly rewarded in your annual evaluation or tenure and promotion process, you should consider carefully how this might affect your other work. Quite simply, this is not an academic activity to be taken on lightly.

But what will those time demands look like? As we have mentioned, prior to the trip, you will spend time talking to administrators; planning the curriculum and itinerary; developing the budget; negotiating with hotels, airlines, and other service providers; as well as recruiting students. Even if you are experienced in all these areas, the process of advertising and promoting the course/trip will take significant energy. We recommend you utilize as many communication avenues as are open to you to get the word out among your students. Having numerous information sessions where you explain to students all aspects of participation is recommended, but you should expect to have to repeat all the same information numerous times in one-on-one sessions with students (and parents) who simply stop by your office, email, or call. Once the registration period opens, you will spend a significant amount of time following up with students who have expressed interest but not yet registered. And for every payment date you have scheduled, you will need to send out reminders, track payments, and then follow up with students who have missed the deadlines.

Many aspects of the course will be similar to your traditional on-ground classes during the semester, although you will undoubtedly spend significant time on the administrative aspects of traveling with students. Given that for most of us, these courses are not part of our regular load, you should not underestimate the time this new course preparation will take. You should also expect that the students will engage in the course material differently than they ordinarily would (as they are about to visit/see the places, people, and things they are studying), which will stimulate questions and discussion for which you need to be prepared and to which you may have to adapt, supplement, or modify your curriculum. This requires a slightly different type of class preparation on the part of the faculty and often a greater depth of preparation.

> While teaching classes on global human rights and European politics in Germany, it became apparent that while our students were aware of concentration camps as a tool of oppression, the magnitude of their horror seemed understated in the academic discussion and hard to imagine. Recognizing this, we chose to have the students watch "Schindler's List" before visiting Dachau. The students were shocked and moved by the images in the film and admitted they had not really "gotten it" prior to watching it. Helping the students put the visit to Dachau into context and facilitating their vision of how it operated really helped make the experience powerful and generated significant discussion on the nature of humanity.

Once you are traveling, you should be prepared for little to no individual or relaxation time. Regardless of how you set up the itinerary, there will be some students who seek to be with you at all times. If you give students time for meals, shopping, etc., you should expect that at least some of them will not be comfortable doing this on their own and will want to accompany you. Even if your students are fairly independent, you will often have to utilize the "off" time given to students to deal with tour guides, hotels, and transportation companies, etc. concerning issues/developments that arise. You should also be prepared to spend more time than you may wish dealing with the students' personal issues. Whether it is someone not feeling well or tensions between roommates, it will become your issue. We have had trips where we spent hours resolving tensions and conflicts between students which arose over incredibly minor events. Don't be surprised if these issues arise late at night. Your students will not hesitate to knock on your hotel room door to ask for your attention and assistance. In this way, study abroad classes are nothing like your on-ground classes, you are not just their instructor, you are their parent for the duration of the trip. These demands can leave the faculty exhausted.

The time demands do not necessarily end once you return to campus. Some campuses/ administrators require post-trip reporting that goes beyond the budgeting requirements of submitting receipts, etc. Some expect reports including course, travel, and site evaluations that can take significant time to prepare. Particularly if you have sought financial support from various entities on campus, you should expect to have to provide some form of report. One key aspect of gaining support for travel activities on campus (as well as raising interest and awareness for future trips) is having your students do public presentations upon returning. Such presentations will be a must if you receive funding from community groups off campus. These activities are great ways to highlight the importance of study abroad and the work you and your students did as well as honor any of the donors, but you will need to handle the coordination. These presentations are most likely going to happen after the course has officially ended, so you should expect to have to do more of the facilitation and coordination for student group presentations than you would if you still had them all in class.

Reintegration

Finally, there is a great deal of research regarding "reverse culture shock" (see Brislin, Cushner, and Yoshida 1997; Gaw 2000; Allison, Davis-Berman, and Berman 2011; Furham 2012 for just a few examples). Students will have had an opportunity to see their world increase in scope, often challenging their view of the world, while their friends and family will be the same as before they left. Your "world travelers" may look to you for how to make sense of their "old world" given their experiences. Be available to them, at the very least by responding to social media messages, e-mails, or phone calls. Ideally, you have helped open up their world. So, you have one last responsibility; help them reintegrate to their home if needed. You will have a shared experience none of their family or friends will have had. Validate the significance of that experience by maintaining communication with them. They will eventually settle into their new normal, but they may need you to help with that transition until they have.

While we have a relatively small campus and are likely to continue to see our students regularly until they graduate, not all faculty will run into the students who they traveled with. If you do not see them (or they have graduated and are no longer around), you can create blogs or social media groups on platforms such as Facebook, Instagram, WhatsApp, GroupMe, or whatever app is popular with your students. You may also want to consider travel reunions or invitations to come back to campus and use the enthusiasm and experience of "peers" to not only validate study abroad among the campus community but recruit for your next study abroad trip.

Asking the Right Questions

There may not be one perfect balance in the distribution of responsibilities but hopefully we have given you some sense of what to expect of the work of course-based study abroad. The key to making a good decision about whether to lead a course-based study abroad trip lies in understanding the balance that exists on your campus. So, start asking questions about who is going to be expected to do what, and use the previous discussion to guide your inquiry.

CHECKLIST

University Responsibility

- Logistics
  - ☐ Approval of instructor/documentation
  - ☐ Approval of tour operators, hotels, and providers
  - ☐ Management of the fees for travel
  - ☐ Management of registration considerations
  - ☐ Management of payments for trip services
  - ☐ International medical and trip insurance
  - ☐ Determination of the student/faculty ratio
  - ☐ Student eligibility
  - ☐ Administrative support

- ☐ Cost, pay, and evaluation
- ☐ Teaching and workload considerations

Faculty Responsibility
- ☐ Coordinating the "stuff"
- ☐ Make sure you are traveling with the right people
- ☐ Understand the time requirements
- ☐ Reintegration
- ☐ Asking the right questions

NOTES

1 Spencer and Tuma state that "The student/faculty ratio should ideally be smaller than that of an on-campus course, as the role of the faculty director extends far beyond the classroom." They go on to suggest that a second faculty or staff member "…can be of tremendous help to the faculty director" (20017, 14–15).

2 Natalee Holloway was a high school student who disappeared in Aruba on a graduation trip with 130 other students in 2005. While legally declared dead, her remains have yet to be found.

REFERENCES

Allison, Peter, Jennifer Davis-Berman, and Dene Berman. 2011. "Changes in Latitude, Changes in Attitude: Analysis of the Effects of Reverse Culture Shock – a Study of Students Returning from Youth Expeditions." *Leisure Studies* 31 (4): 487–503.

BBC News. 2010. "How Volcano Chaos Unfolded: in Graphics." *BBC*, April, 21. http://news.bbc.co.uk/2/hi/europe/8634944.stm (Accessed September 8, 2018).

Brislin, Richard W., Kenneth Cushner, and Tomoko Yoshida. 1997. *Improving Intercultural Interactions*. Thousand Oaks, CA: Sage Publications, Inc.

Furham, Adrian. 2012. "Culture Shock." *Journal of Psychology and Education* 7 (1): 9–22.

Gaw, Kenneth F. 2000. "Reverse Culture Shock in Students Returning from Overseas." *International Journal of Intercultural Relations* 24: 83–104.

Harris, Richard. 2010. "Tracking Volcano Ash to Improve Flight Safety." *NPR, All Things Considered*, April, 22. www.npr.org/templates/story/story.php?storyId=126195002 (Accessed September 8, 2018).

Spencer, Sarah E. and Kathy Tuma, eds. 2017. *The Guide to Successful Short-Term Programs Abroad*. Washington, DC: NAFSA.

Chapter Seven

So, Are You Ready?

You have planned the trip, recruited the students, you are very excited and want to make this the best travel experience possible. But wait! Are you really ready? Are the students? Are you sure you (and they) know all that you need about the country that you are traveling to? In this chapter, we will discuss what you need to review with the students (and confirm for yourself) before you get on the plane. This chapter explains the pre-departure review that faculty should conduct in order to ensure that once on ground all goes smoothly. From familiarity with the destination and the current political, social, and economic conditions, logistics, alerting cell carriers and credit card companies of your travel plans, whether cash or credit is preferred and how to get cash (or if you should bring it), learning how everyone's medical and travel insurance will work in the country to determining the safety/legality issues of the locations to be visited as well as the legality of common student activities, the details of what you should know are outlined in the following.

KNOW THE COUNTRY

You spent all this time doing the research on the country(ies) you selected and preparing your class, but how well do you really know the country you are traveling to? Optimally you would like to understand the country as well as someone who lives there as you are really acting as a host for your students. So, before you head to the airport, make sure you are comfortable with a few aspects effecting travel and operations in your selected country. You should consider, first, the current political, social, and economic conditions; second, the contemporary social and cultural norms; and, finally, the logistical information relevant to your trip.

The political, social, and economic conditions in any country vary over time. Whether it is heightened racial tensions or acceptance of certain types of behavior, we can see differences even in the U.S. across regions and time. You will

SO, ARE YOU READY?

want to make sure you fully understand the conditions in the places you will travel so that you can assist your students in dealing with these factors. Information on current political, social, and economic conditions can be found from any number of travel websites, but your first and most important information source is the U.S. State Department website, which has information for U.S. citizens traveling to foreign countries. This will include information on safety issues; current political system and status; and economic data, such as the type of commerce to expect, as well as explanations of the social norms concerning public behavior. Other sources will be websites and promotional materials from the governments and tourist/visitor bureaus of the countries and cities you are traveling to.

You will have provided your students a broad understanding of the history and culture of the country through the history books, novels, movies, and other resources that you used for your classes before travel. But it is also important to have specific information on the culture and social norms in the country, as well as specific states and regions you will be visiting. Again, hopefully you will have discussed this with your students beforehand, but it is always a good idea to check for the most current information before you leave and review this with the students. Many travel websites offer advice on social norms and expectations concerning appropriate dress and behavior. Consult these sites to ensure that you are well aware of the current standards. You will need to prepare (and continue to consult while traveling) your students on appropriate attire, how to interact with the local population, and what to expect, so the more information you have, the better. You should remind students about what kinds of behaviors or attire may be acceptable in the U.S. and the students take for granted but may not be where you are going. You do not want your students to accidentally offend anyone or engage in activities that are unwelcome. Be it table manners, behavior in public places, or the role of women, it is important for everyone to be aware of how the culture will operate in the places you will visit. Students should also understand that they are representing their institution, their faculty, and country. So, their behavior is important.

Understanding the logistics specific to your trip is key to ensuring smooth travel. While you have prepared all aspects of the itinerary and discussed the key elements with your students, there are a couple of logistical considerations we recommend you review and remind students of, immediately before departure.

First, you want to make sure each student (and you, of course) has a hard copy of all the key information concerning the trip. This information should include flight information, hotel information, the name and contact information of your tour agent (if you are using one), the itinerary, and emergency contact numbers

SO, ARE YOU READY?

(including the "911" number of the destinations you will be visiting since there is no universal emergency number) as well as the contact information for each student while traveling. You will want to make sure each student also has and brings with them throughout the trip a hard copy of their insurance information in case they need to reference it at any time and when they are not with you. Don't rely on electronic copies of the information as accessing information saved on cell phones or stored in emails may be impossible in certain areas or at certain times (like when those students forget to charge their phones). You will want to make sure the students pass along this information to their families as well. Students should also be reminded that they should record the relevant information from their credit cards and passport—and leave this information at home—so that if they were to lose these items, reporting it to the relevant parties would be as easy as possible.

We recommend that you carry a hard copy of the picture page of each student's passport with you as well as copies of their insurance information and emergency contact information for use in case of emergency. This should be kept with you each day as you travel. The U.S. medical system and payment procedures are likely to be very different from where you are traveling. It is best to familiarize yourself with what to expect if you do need medical attention for your students or yourself while abroad and what your medical insurance will pay for (and whether the insurance will handle all the payments or if you will have to pay and then get reimbursed). Be sure to know what kind of documentation you will need for your insurance plan, so you are not having to call, email, fax, etc. overseas for information needed to process any claims.

Additionally, you should have the contact information (with local phone numbers) for your tour agent and specific information on who is picking you up at the airport, etc. Invariably, if you arrive after a long international flight and don't know exactly who you are looking for at pickup, you will spend more time than you (or the students) would wish locating your contact, so make sure you know who is supposed to be there and how to contact them (at whatever hour you arrive). If you are starting to think that you may end up dragging a large folder of information around throughout your trip that most likely you won't need, you are probably right. But trust us, you will be very glad to have all that information on you if it turns out you need it!

You will also want to make sure you understand your travel insurance. Travel insurance can cover a wide range of travel issues from flight cancellations to travel disruptions caused by forces outside your control. Know what your travel insurance covers, so you make sure you are taking advantage of all of the benefits you are paying for. If your flight gets canceled, does your

SO, ARE YOU READY?

insurance pay for room and board while you await re-ticketing if the delay is for an extended time? Are there provisions for "natural causes," such as tornados or hurricanes, or labor actions such as strikes or work slowdowns which your travel insurance will not accept as a reason for a claim? Is there coverage if you miss a flight because of long lines, slow traffic, etc.? Know the specifics of your plan before you leave. Don't just assume you can call or figure it out if you need to. A natural disaster that grounds air travel could also take out telecommunication capabilities. Being prepared by knowing the details of your travel insurance plan can make a travel disruption an annoyance rather than a catastrophe.

Immediately before departure you will want to contact your cell phone carrier to set up international coverage. As most carriers charge for this additional service by the number of days it is active, you will want to wait until you are ready to leave to initiate the service. (Invariably, if you do this too far ahead of time, it will be turned on too early and you will end up paying more than you hoped.) When you contact your carrier, get instructions as to how to use your phone in the various locations you will be traveling. Frequently, carriers require that you call or text a certain number upon arrival (or initial usage) in a country which acts as an agreement to the fees and service charges related to use in that specific country. The process for making local calls or even calls back to the U.S. may require the use of international country codes or some other access process, so make sure you and the students review these immediately prior to travel. You should also confirm that all the students have this information for their carriers as well as your contact information stored in their phones and on a hard copy before you leave. As mentioned previously, this is something you should have gone over in class, but you will want to refresh your memory and remind your students about the process and possible costs for using their phones abroad.

One aspect of traveling with students which often surprises people is how much of their time is spent dealing with financial issues. Not only will you be responsible for making sure the group expenses (which were not pre-paid) are covered, but you will also spend time counseling the students on when, where, and how to get cash and exchange currency. Hopefully, the University has provided a credit or debit card for your use on the trip and pre-paid much of the fixed expenses. You should make sure to call the credit card company to notify them of the dates and locations of travel. Failing to do so will likely result in them denying charges, so you want to make sure to remind your students of this as well. You will also want to make sure you understand if there are transaction or foreign currency fees or daily spending/cash limits on the cards.

SO, ARE YOU READY?

Despite all this, you will find that a substantial portion of your (and the student's) expenditures will need to be done in cash. Most likely, it will be significantly more than you do at home, as many countries do not rely on credit cards to the degree we do in the U.S. That means you are going to have to carry a substantial amount of cash. Determining how much you need to have on hand can vary by the country you are visiting (and the accessibility of ATMs, etc.) and the types of activities planned for any given day. If you are planning on visiting rural villages, attending a street fair, or an artisan's market, you should expect all your spending to have to be done in cash. No matter where you are traveling, expect to have to pay for the entrance to many historical sites, tips for service providers, and daily expenditures like snacks and drinks in cash. You will need to remind your students immediately before travel (and throughout the trip) how much cash they should have.

You should have discussed issues of personal security with your students in the class/sessions prior to travel but you should also remind them in the days before you leave that they should be cognizant of the safety of each member of the group, particularly because everyone will be carrying a significant amount of cash. We also suggest that you utilize your students as security aids for yourself and the other instructors who may be carrying a large amount of cash for the group. Either distribute some of the group cash across the students (so that if one of you has something stolen, you don't lose everything) or at least ask the students to be aware that you have all the cash and they need to help look out for you and your bags. Once you reach your hotel, you can deposit most of your cash in the hotel or room safe, but when you are carrying significant amounts, asking the students to be aware of that and assist you in keeping an eye out is a very good idea.

And remember that you will need to collect receipts for virtually every cent you spend, whether in cash or on credit. We suggest that you take with you a small notebook in which you can make notes as to where you ate, what you bought, and what you spent each day, along with a designated envelope or folder in which you can keep the receipts as you travel. By the time you return and sit down to do your accounting, having notes to remind you of your meals and purchases by day will be a tremendous help as those receipts you kept could be in a foreign language and will almost certainly be in a non-U.S. currency.

SAFETY AND LEGALITY CONSIDERATIONS

There are vast differences in how societies operate around the world and it will be your responsibility while traveling to ensure that the students are safe and do not run into any legal issues. So, when it comes to safety and legality concerns, please do not count on the students remembering what you said in class. At this point, they are almost ready to leave and are excited about the upcoming departure. So, you will want to remind them of the behavioral expectations you have set for them. You should remind them of your policies concerning personal behavior (which can encompass everything from speaking in a soft voice in certain religious sites to sexual activity), the consumption of alcohol and tobacco, as well as issues such as to what is illegal in the country you are going to that wouldn't be in the U.S. (e.g., camouflage attire, swearing, head coverings—really!). You should also review actions, which all the students know to be illegal, but may have significantly different penalties in some countries, such as the illegal possession of marijuana.

No matter your comfort level with a country, the number of times you have visited before, or the amount of research you did for the class/advance sessions with students, it is important that you check on the travel conditions in the days before you travel. Since situations in countries can quickly change, it is advisable to monitor travel advisories. We suggest that you follow the U.S. Department of State: Consular Affairs Facebook and travel.state.gov Twitter (@Travelogue) pages, which can provide real time updates on conditions in country.

You will also want to remind your students to register on the State Department webpage (if they have not already done so in one of your class sessions) and make sure all the instructors/group leaders are familiar with your university's emergency plan and procedures for travelers.

CONCLUSION

Like many other academic endeavors, preparation goes a long way in guaranteeing success of your course-based study abroad experience. You will soon be leading a group of students who are going to be very excited, anxious, and nervous about the trip, so you, as faculty, will have to be organized, confident, and levelheaded while making all the decisions. The information you collected and presented (numerous times) to your students will enable you and your students to handle whatever may come. Traveling to a new country is always a challenge and more so with a group of young adults. This pre-departure work will not only have left you better prepared but will also have given your students information they will need to handle the cultural differences, and the uncertainty of being far from home. Knowing about the country, its culture, and the people will make the trip even more interesting as you and your students will look forward to seeing and experiencing all that you have learned.

SO, ARE YOU READY?

CHECKLIST

- ☐ Know the country
- ☐ Logistics
- ☐ Alerting cell carriers and credit card companies of your travel plans
- ☐ Cash or credit?
- ☐ Medical and travel insurance
- ☐ Receipts
- ☐ Safety and legality considerations

Chapter Eight

On Ground

You made it! After a year of envisioning this trip and months of recruiting and planning you are finally in country. This is exciting but also a little daunting, especially if this is your first visit to the country. You start checking your mental to do list before even the plane lands: getting the students through customs and immigration, collecting all your bags (hopefully they all made it), coordinating some money exchange for yourself and the students and locating your tour agent or ride to the hotel. You exit the airport and it all begins. You are in a whirlwind that will not stop until you get home. In this chapter, we outline what your on-ground experience is likely to be. We begin with a discussion of dealing with the students when on the trip. We focus on the need to keep students informed about the daily plan, and remind them about the day's activities and considerations, as well as the nuances of in-country travel, and the artificial comfort some students will develop in country which can influence their behavior.

While it is very exciting to see all your plans come to fruition, you may quickly realize that your role is going to be very different than it ordinarily is on your home campus. As a secondary focus of this chapter, we consider what to do when you realize that there are things you did not think about or foresee happening to you or your group. It will be up to you as the faculty leader to make sure you maintain your composure at all times, adapt, and find solutions to anything that might come up. Remember the role of the faculty is part mentor, part parent, part teacher, and part drill sergeant and it's up to you to know when to assume what role.

AS SOON AS YOU LAND

The pilot has announced that you are landing soon, and the flight attendants have given out immigration forms. This will be your first "on ground" task, and you can start doing it in the air. You should have advised your students to have a blue or black ink pen with them on the plane as many customs agencies will not accept forms completed in other colors, but you should be prepared with extra pens to share. You will undoubtedly need to explain to students how to fill out the form. We suggest you have a handout ready with the address and contact numbers of where you will be staying. This question will be on the immigration form and we guarantee it will flummox your students. You should list the hotel where you will be staying (or, if you are traveling to multiple cities, the hotel of the first city) or, if you have a tour company or travel agent on ground, their address.

Once off the plane, the next step is to herd the group through customs and immigration. The customs and immigration process will vary by country and you will need to have a rough idea of how this is done. Many airlines, as well as customs and immigration websites (www.immihelp.com) have sample forms posted for travel to various countries. Familiarize yourself with the forms so you can explain the process and documents needed to the students. Most of your students will be unfamiliar with the process of going through immigration and customs and many of them are likely to be a bit intimidated. While most government websites do not list sample questions that an immigration officer might ask, travel websites and blogs can shed some light on that. Hopefully, you discussed this process in class prior to traveling but you will need to remind students of their visa status. Undoubtedly, you are all traveling on tourist visas so when asked, students should indicate that, even though this trip is a part of their academic coursework. "Student" visas are issued only to those enrolled in a country's educational institutions and entail significant documentation requirements, so you have to tell your group that if asked the "purpose of their visit" they should say tourism, instead of study so as to reduce any confusion.

Make sure to tell your students that they should be prepared for biometrics such as having their fingerprints or picture taken, or their retina's scanned. These first interactions with governmental officials of another country can be confusing and intimidating, especially for the first-time traveler, so you want to make sure the students understand the process and do not get nervous and/or give the wrong answers, which might cause unnecessary delays.

You will also want to tell your students to have their passport and customs form in their hands ready to go. In many places if they approach the customs agent with an incomplete form they will be sent to the back of the line, thus possibly delaying your group. Your on-ground guide or agent will only be able to meet you after you exit the airport, so they will not be able to assist you. All the members of your group should have the same information for the customs officials on the purpose of the trip, how long they will be staying, what cities they will be visiting, and where they will be staying. They may not all be asked those questions, but it is good to have that information on hand as they are very common inquiries. Make sure to explain to the students that they will have to go through immigration and customs individually. Some students may become a bit intimidated and try to go through in groups. This may cause the customs agent to send one or more of the students back, and in some cases, we have seen them yell at the offending parties. Immigration and Customs officials are trained to be extra-vigilant and do not have much patience with people who do not follow rules. They expect the traveler to know what to do, be prepared to answer their questions, and have all the correct and required paperwork ready. This often can be disconcerting when there are language differences, and it is especially intimidating for first time travelers.

When traveling with multiple faculty members, make sure you stagger your own processing through customs and immigration, with one faculty member being the first of your group to go through and one last, after all the students have made it through. In most customs and immigration processing areas, individuals are not permitted to wait for other passengers after having been reviewed and they are required to move outside the area. If you stagger the processing of faculty, and there are any issues or delays, there will be someone with each group of students. If you are the only faculty member or chaperone with the group, make sure you are the last to go through and that students wait for you at the next place they are permitted to wait.

Now on to baggage claim. Depending on the airport, this can be a bit chaotic so make sure you are there with all the students (and no one has wandered off to the bathroom or something) and that all the students collect all their own bags. Having common luggage tags (some universities give out luggage tags with the university logo to those traveling as part of a course) or some common marker will help to identify the bags, making it easy for all the students to participate in grabbing bags and speeding up the process. Some airports have luggage trolleys available for free, others charge. No matter what, it is a good idea to have a few trolleys to make the movement through the airport and out to your ground transport a little faster, since students will likely be tired and juggling more than one bag.

We are all aware of cases of baggage mishandling by airlines, and how sometimes your luggage does not arrive with you. This can be very disconcerting and troublesome, especially on an international trip where you plan on moving from city to city. Always advise your students to pack a change of clothing and essentials, including valuables and medication in their carry-ons, so that they can manage for a day or two, if there is a delay in the luggage arriving.

> We had this happen when we went to the Caribbean. There was only one flight a day from the U.S. to the island, so we had to wait 24 hours for our bags. Luckily, we had told students to bring necessities in carry-ons. So, everyone had swimsuits etc., and no one had to miss out on some beach time the next day, while we waited for our bags.

After you have claimed your baggage, there is one more stop before you exit the airport: currency exchange. Although airport currency exchange booths may give you a less favorable exchange rate than locations outside the airport, they are convenient, and it is a good idea to have at least some amount of the local currency from the outset of your trip.

You should have discussed with students ahead of time that few merchants will accept the U.S. Dollars for transactions and in some places, it is illegal to use a currency other than the local currency for purchases. We find that we have to be explicit about this with our students, as many of them have traveled to Mexico or parts of the Caribbean where U.S. currency is so desirable that it is often accepted in lieu of the local currency. Perhaps more importantly, not all places take credit or debit cards—students will have to have cash. You will need your passport, and sometimes your boarding pass, to exchange your currency. So, keep that handy, along with the amount of money you want to exchange. You have a large group and it often takes several minutes for each person to conduct an exchange. If you don't want to be there for an excruciatingly long time, tell students to be prepared.

The exchange rates are written on the information boards or signs at the currency exchange vendor. Consult these to ensure you receive the right amount before you leave the counter. Also, remember to tell your students that there is a fee for currency exchanges. You will likely also be able to exchange money at your hotel, but the fees charged may be more than at the airports or outside vendors. Your local guide should be able to give you information about where to find better rates and exchange fees once you get going, but for your immediate needs, the airport currency exchange will be convenient. Now you are ready to exit the airport. This is when the customs officials will collect the Customs Declaration forms. It is unlikely you will need to declare anything, but if you are uncertain the customs declaration form explains the requirements for declaring goods or cash for the country you are entering. In many countries, customs procedures for arriving international passengers are differentiated based on what you have to declare. This distinction is often designated by color coded signs and channels. Passengers who have nothing to declare (carrying goods that are within the permitted lists and limits and not prohibited) go through the one channel (usually designated as green), while passengers carrying items to declare (above the permitted limits or beyond the prohibited list) will have to go through another (usually designated as red). Inform your students that countries treat these customs rules very seriously, so they should be cognizant of where they should go.

> Entry into a particular channel constitutes a legal declaration, if a passenger going through the green channel is found to be carrying goods above the customs limits or prohibited items, he or she may be prosecuted for making a false declaration to customs, by virtue of having gone through the green channel. Each channel is a point of no return, and once a passenger has entered a particular channel, they cannot go back.
> (World Customs Organization 2018)

Once you exit the airport, locate your guide or your pickup. If you have not arranged for private transportation, you should have already put together information for public transport, such as cabs, buses, local trains (Metro, Tube, etc.). Many airports will also have information on pre-paid transportation, such as shuttles and taxis, which can be quite handy for those new to a country. Airports in Asian countries will have booths marked Pre-Paid Transportation where you can book and pre-pay for the cab or shuttle before you exit the airport. You are asked for your destination and contact information, as well as group size, and you are assigned a vehicle which you pay for at the booth. You will be then directed to the vehicle driver, to whom you hand the pre-paid receipt. For a first-time visitor to a city, this allows you to travel safely to your hotel, preventing bargaining for fares, price gouging, or confusion caused by the passengers and drivers not speaking the same language. Since the pre-paid counter has your information and gives you the license plate number of the vehicle, as well as driver information, the driver will not be able to take you or your group for a ride in a new destination.

If you have pre-arranged private transportation, ahead of time, such as a private coach or bus for your group, expect the driver or guide will likely have the name of your group or your name as the faculty leader on a placard. They will usually be waiting for you at the exit of the customs area and should have told you in advance exactly where to find them. If you have arranged for a bus to pick your group up, you will then have to get your luggage to the bus and load it onto the bus. This is likely going to be the first of many times you will have to do this over the course of your trip (if you are traveling between cities) so make sure that the students identify their bags as they are being loaded onto the bus and they do not get on the bus until they see the bags being loaded. In some countries of Asia, it is not unusual for there to be an assistant on the bus who is responsible for loading and unloading luggage. Everyone in your group will be required to identify their

ON GROUND

bags before loading and after unloading to make sure their bags have arrived at the destination. This is a common expectation of the transportation companies and an important step to make sure bags are not lost or stolen. In some places this is also considered a security requirement to make sure no unaccounted for bags are included with those of your group. This is a rule that is followed at every stop throughout the trip and is also the case when you arrive at the hotel. Even if this is not a custom or expectation in the country where you are traveling, make it one for your group. It is just a good way to make sure no one loses a bag.

Once you are on the bus, if you have a guide, he/she will likely give you and your students a little welcome speech and tell you about the city that you are entering, pointing out highlights on the way. Instruct your students to be courteous and respectful to the guide, and to pay attention, even though they may be tired after many hours of travel and not in the mood. Not only are these the moments when first impressions are made—this is also the time when the guide will likely lay out the basic framework for rules and procedures for the trip. You want your students to get this information and begin the process of developing a good working relationship with your guide.

Once you arrive at your hotel, you still have some important business to conduct so don't let the students wander off or simply lounge around the lobby. In most cases, the hotel will have prior information of your arrival time and will be ready to receive you, but you will need to present the passports for all guests in order to check in. We have found if you collect all the passports for the hotel staff and then distribute the room keys/assignments to your students the process will move much faster than if you have each student check in separately. Most students are eager to check in and go to their rooms, so the more you can expedite the check-in process the happier the students are. Many hotels, especially in India, will have a welcome drink and a welcome ceremony for foreign tourists. This can be very refreshing after the long flight and introduces the students to the culture and hospitality of the country, but it is something students do not tend to expect so you will want to explain this to them and ask them to be polite (even though they may be exhausted).

The hotel should have a rooming list ready if you have sent information on your group ahead of time and will have placed the students with their roommates in the appropriate rooms. You will want to get a copy of this list with room numbers and share it with each faculty member and your guide. That way, if you have to find one of the students, you will know what room they are in. Inform the students that they cannot change roommates once they arrive at their destination. These decisions should have been made ahead of time and should not be changed as this is the list the hotel, you, and guides will use if there is a question about accountability.

While checking in at the hotel, please make sure you take charge, so that the students understand the information about the hotel (such as the Wi-Fi code and location of the breakfast room), rules, and restrictions, and also tell them to let you know if things are not working in the rooms. Sometimes, despite the best efforts of housekeeping at the hotels, there are problems in the rooms. The students need to let you (and/or the tour company) know so you have a sense of the overall situation and can negotiate with the hotel if things are not resolved. The sooner these issues are reported, the sooner they can be addressed, and the more pleasant the stay will be for everyone.

Hotels should also have Wi-Fi information they will give to the students. Optimally, they will have a card or information sheet to give to each guest upon check in, but if not, you should expect to have to relay this information—multiple times. Depending on your destination and the hotel policy, there may be a charge to use the Wi-Fi and you should inform the students that this is a charge that is not included in the price of their room (assuming you were not able to negotiate that ahead of time). They will need to be prepared to pay the charges at check-out. Don't forget to remind the students about the costs of using the mini-bars and laundry as well as other incidentals for which they are responsible.

Once checked in, students are often in a hurry to get to their room to lay down or unpack. But before you let them go, make sure you go over the details for the rest of the day or, if this is the end of the day, the next day. Inform them about the schedule, when and where to meet for breakfast, what to wear, what to carry with them, etc. Also, make sure that all the students have your room number and contact information, are signed in on the common messaging app, and know to let you know if they need anything. You should make sure your students know the name and location of their hotel. Hotels in many countries will have business cards available at the front desk with the name of the hotel and its address in English and the local language, which can be shown to cabdrivers, etc. to ease the language barrier. This can be tremendously helpful if the students are ever lost or traveling by themselves.

These are small things but very important. Don't rely on the fact that you went over all these things in class or take for granted that the students will read the daily schedule and know what to do. Remember they are in a different country, different time zone, tired, and dazed after a long flight. You are too, but it is your job to make sure all goes well from the first day on.

COMMITMENT TO THE ITINERARY

So, you are about to begin all the activities you have been planning for so long. We know you are excited about all the sites and the possibilities they hold, but

ON GROUND

don't forget you have a commitment to keep to the itinerary as planned. You have to honor the promises you made to the students when they signed up for the class and trip. So, make sure everyone (students, guides, etc.) understands that, and are very conscientious about staying on schedule. So, if you have set a specific time to leave the hotel for the day's activities, explain to students that you expect to be able to walk out the door at that time. They should be standing in front of you five minutes before that time, not just heading to the elevator to come downstairs. Trust us, if you are not strict on the schedule you will find each day it takes longer and longer to get your group moving as people become more lackadaisical about being on time and eventually this will take a toll on your ability to accomplish the day's activities.

We strongly suggest that you get the students up and going on your daily itinerary as soon as possible. Plan your itinerary so that the students can start activities immediately upon arrival (if it is not late at night). They will likely be tired from international air travel, and wish to sleep late that first morning, but don't give in to this temptation. The sooner they get up and get going, the sooner they will get used to the time difference. This also sets the tone for the purpose of the travel: learning, and not vacation. As an added bonus, it pretty much guarantees they will make it an early night that first night.

The students have to keep up with the itinerary and be ready (and physically able) to do all the activities you have planned. You should have created an itinerary that balances giving the students enough time to rest, while at the same time taking advantage of the time you have in country. Keep them busy most of the time. We say this not to take the fun and adventure out of the trip but to keep the academic focus of the trip front and center rather than allowing it to be just an expensive tourist experience. If there is free time in the schedule due to factors outside of your control, then consider offering suggestions for optional activities for the students. Just make sure you set a designated time to check back in with you so that you can be sure everyone is back and ready for the rest of the group activities. For example, when we travel to Ranthambore Tiger Reserve, the tours out into the park occur only in the early morning and at dusk due to the heat. This means that students are left with several hours in the middle of the day with no programmed activities. We permit students to spend time at the pool, rest in their rooms, or visit a local market. The only requirement is that everyone is back and ready to go on the afternoon safari. No matter how you set up your itinerary, try to make sure they are back in the hotel at a reasonable hour to rest (if they do not sleep once they are in, it is their fault). Start them off **early** every day, as this sets the tone of an academic endeavor and will make sure you get to accomplish the itinerary for the day. You don't want to get off schedule and miss something or be subject to factors such as the weather or traffic which are determined by the time of day and which you worked hard to plan to avoid. For example, for our trips to India, we regularly plan the itinerary such that we do as much sightseeing (that requires us to be outdoors) as possible early in the day, before it gets too hot (temperatures in May can easily hit 100°F by noon), but this requires leaving the hotel by 8:00 a.m. After lunch, we try go to places indoors, such as museums or monuments where it will be cooler.

If the hotel provides breakfast, at least the first day in each hotel, require that the students meet you for breakfast by a certain hour. We suggest that you meet at least an hour before the departure time as this will force them to get out of bed, get past some of their jetlag, and overcome any uncertainties they have about how the buffet works, etc. You can use this time to make sure everyone is up and running, as well as remind the group of the activities of the day.

Throughout your travels, you will have to remind the students that they are on a tight schedule. In order to accomplish all the activities they were looking forward to, students have to understand the importance of being on the move at all times. This means efficient check-in and check-out at hotels, not straying from the group when walking between locations, etc. They have to be aware of the time so that they can get the most out of the time spent in every location. Therefore, the evening briefings and reminders become very important.

While you should keep to the itinerary as much as possible, there may be times when you have to adjust the schedule. When this occurs, everyone (students, faculty, and tour agents) needs to be flexible. This is not an uncommon development when traveling from one city to another, and flights/trains are delayed. Delays such as this may cause you to have to re-order events on the itinerary. If you are working with a tour agent, they should be prepared to handle these incidents. Make sure to notify your tour agent immediately if you experience a travel disruption or delay, if they don't have someone traveling with you. The sooner they know about the issues, the sooner they can make the appropriate adjustments. If you are coordinating this on your own, you will need to be prepared to shuffle the itinerary. Hopefully, you have considered some options ahead of time, but if not, you can always consult with your hotel staff about how to accomplish your itinerary. Students have to learn to adapt and adjust when these things happen: even if that means they have to spend a little less time at some site or get up early the next day to accommodate the new schedule. Students will be much more understanding (although disappointed) when something has to change due to factors outside your control if the management of the trip is such that they are not missing things because of things you can control (others are late, etc.). Accordingly, it is very important that you keep them informed about what is happening and what you are doing to give them what was promised in the itinerary.

THE EVENING BRIEFING

As mentioned earlier, we suggest that you have a meeting every evening, as soon as you reach the hotel, before the students disperse for the night, or schedule a **required** meeting at a set time every evening. These meetings are necessary to reflect on the day's activities as well as provide an opportunity so that you can brief them on the next day's program, activities, clothing requirements, and departure time for the next day. This is also a good time to check with the students individually and as a group to see how things are going. You will want to encourage them to let you know about any issues they might have. It is a good idea to have these conversations (especially with the first-time travelers) since they may have things that they need to discuss and not know how or the best time to talk to you. This is also a time to have a discussion with the students about the day's activities you just completed, get a sense of their impressions of what they have seen and how they are enjoying the trip. Try to gauge the students' excitement as well as exhaustion levels. You may need to be very perceptive about the students' moods and feelings, so you can help resolve any issues as soon as you notice them. Optimally you should be the first one to know when something is not right, but sometimes students are hesitant to share their concerns. If you remind them at the evening briefings that part of the learning process is thinking about what they see and experience, as well as to "check in" with everyone you may find that the students will seek you out privately for more serious concerns. We once had the experience of learning about disturbing (and illegal) behavior among the students from these mandatory daily briefings. Only when prompted to let us know how things were going did some of the women on the trip inform us that one of the young men was sexually harassing and physically intimidating them.

As discussed in "What to Teach," your syllabus should contain a reflection component which asks students to process what they learned during the day or in a visit to a specific monument or site. Regardless of what form this assignment or activity takes in your class, the evening briefings provide the perfect opportunity for students to begin some of the reflection work. We strongly suggest you hold these sessions in the evening for a couple of reasons. If you attempt to do these first thing in the morning, you will frequently find that students are more focused on the upcoming activities as opposed to considering yesterday's experiences, or they oversleep and miss the discussion. If you have them in the middle of the day (perhaps while on the bus traveling between sites when you have downtime), you will likely find it difficult to get everyone to switch gears from sightseeing to contemplation. And if you provide information about the next day's expectations during a mid-day meeting, you will likely find that the students forget what you told them as they enjoy the remainder of the day's activities. Finally, by holding the sessions in the evening you can ensure that everyone is back in the hotel, has thought about where/with whom they will have dinner (if relevant) and you can find out about any other evening plans they might be contemplating (trust us, that is something you will WANT to know). Most importantly, it creates a perfect space to decompress and think about the day's experience.

GROUP DYNAMICS

A positive group dynamic can make for a truly wonderful experience however, there are many things that might disrupt the group dynamic. You do not want unhappiness (whether due to interpersonal issues within the group, issues with the hotel or other factors) to fester and build over the course of the trip. The sooner you deal with these issues and move past them, the better the overall experience—for everyone. One of the most common issues to develop is roommate conflicts. Students may have been the best of friends the whole semester, but the moment they get to a different country, they hate each other and don't want to be roommates any more. You definitely don't want to get caught in a never-ending game of roommate changes, but you also don't want them screaming at each other all night. (Yes, we have seen this happen.) So, there may be cases where you have to make arrangements to move a student to another room; provide them a single room; or, in extreme cases, have them share a room with a faculty until other arrangements can be made.

> We once had an experience in which we had three young men share a room. Two had been friends for years and they decided they did not care for the other student. Assuming the third student did not speak Spanish (which he did), they continually said disparaging things about him in his presence, making him feel entirely unwelcome and uncomfortable. This started the first night of the trip and quickly escalated to become unbearable and was likely going to lead to significant conflict. We had to temporarily move the young man into one of the faculty member's rooms until we could arrange for a private room for him.

These roommate issues may often strike you as silly, and ridiculous. We guarantee at some point you will consider them an unnecessary hassle, and they may even end up causing you to incur additional costs of an extra room. But sometimes these adjustments will be necessary to keep the peace. You may want to remind students that if there are cost implications for their inability to get along, they may be passed on to the particular students.

An additional group dynamic you can expect to face is the development of cliques. Some students bond well with a few people but don't find anything in common with other members of the group. As long as these exclusive groups are not in conflict with each other, they are fine, but if they cause tension, you have to speak to all the members and let them know that this is a class activity, and everyone should be on their best behavior. You may end up intentionally forcing them into different sub-groups as you do your daily activities to encourage them to get to know/include all the members of the class. As faculty you have to make an extra effort to ensure you are dividing your time and attention among all the students and addressing all concerns impartially and equally. These inter-personal dynamics can take on much greater significance when the students spend 24 hours a day together than they would in your traditional classroom setting and as such can become a major distraction if not addressed.

Group dynamics can also be affected when issues arise with the hotel or tour guides. Many of these can be attributed to cultural differences, misunderstanding, or language barriers that cause confusion for the hotel staff, tour guides, or students. At a minimum, this will create a distance between those trying to communicate with your group and may cause your students to discount the message. In some cases, it can also lead to a lack of respect on the part of your students, which is unacceptable. On the other end of the spectrum, you also want to be attuned to inappropriate relationships or interactions between the tour or hotel employees and your students. Particularly if you are working with the same individuals for an extended period, the students may relax or become overly familiar with the staff and then end up in uncomfortable, inappropriate, or even dangerous situations. We once had a situation in which some of the male employees of our hotel befriended the young ladies in our group and eventually the women felt very uncomfortable as the men asked for "hugs" on the day we left. When caught alone with the hotel staff, these "hugs" felt significantly more like sexual embraces to the women and frightened them. As faculty, you have to be the mediator in all instances and in these cases utilize the hotel manager or the tour company to address the problem. Furthermore, you must model/advise your students on the need for professionalism even while being open and friendly to others. Just about all cultural differences can be solved with a little patience and potential issues avoided with a little forethought and discretion but realize that you will have to manage these instances for the group.

CULTURAL UNDERSTANDING AND ON GROUND DYNAMICS

As mentioned previously, the evening briefings will prepare the students for the next day's itinerary. Remind the students to be dressed appropriately and what that means for the places you will visit. If they are going to a religious site, church, temple, or mosque, they should dress modestly and carry a head scarf (or other appropriate head covering) with them that the need for head covering is not always the case, for only women. When visiting the Golden Temple in Amritsar, India, men are asked to cover their heads as well as the women. Some of our male students did not remember to bring their scarves or handkerchiefs with them, but luckily, they had some at the temple for the men to use and they were not refused entry.

Appropriate clothing often includes the need to wear comfortable shoes and appropriate clothes for the weather. Some students will be more focused on looking good for each other than on the demands of the day. If this goes too far, you can have all kinds of issues arise, from sunburn to injuries, and not be able to keep to your itinerary.

> Once, while traveling in Washington D.C., students had been told they had to dress professionally as the group was going to meet with various members of Congress. Despite being briefed about the problems of high heels that were not yet broken in or which were too high, a couple of the young ladies chose to wear shoes based on their appearance rather than practicality. After only a couple of hours (and with many hours remaining in the day's activities), they had blisters all over their feet and could barely walk. While we stopped and bought them Band-Aids, we could not go back to the hotel and let them change, or we would have missed out on several of the items on the itinerary. For the remainder of the trip, they had issues walking long distances; it definitely dampened their experience.

You also have to make sure the group understands the behavioral expectations and cultural norms of the country they are traveling in. What we consider modest or commonly acceptable clothing (i.e., sleeveless blouses) in the U.S. may be considered a bit revealing in other places. Add to that cultural differences about how men and women interact in public and you have a recipe for tension/unhappiness. More than once we have had the experience where men openly stare/leer at or "cat call" some of the female students—even when they dress appropriately. Even if everyone in your group is dressed modestly, you will stick out somewhat. A large group of young people, clearly behaving as tourists will

ON GROUND

draw attention. Aggressive behavior toward women is more commonplace in some cultures than in the U.S. and is only exacerbated by inappropriate attire. You will need to coach your students as to how they should deal with such a situation if it were to arise. Invariably this surprises, scares, and exasperates the students. You don't want these culture clashes to taint the students' view of the country or its people, so it's best to prepare to avoid this.

If you are traveling by public transport, explaining cultural norms may be particularly important. Tell the students to be alert at all times and make sure that they stay with the group. In many places, people cram into buses/subways, not hesitating to bump into or touch others. This is often disconcerting to U.S. students because of different understandings of personal space and can cause them to become uncomfortable or get separated from each other or the group. It is a good idea to divide the students into groups of two or three and to make sure they keep an eye out for their partner. You should also make sure to discuss a plan with your students about what they should do if they get separated from the group. We once "lost" a student who failed to get off the subway at the correct stop in Berlin. Luckily, he ran to the next stop and met the group (who had exited and waited for him) there.

The first test of your students' cultural adaptability usually comes when they are visiting a tourist site like a monument, a memorial, or even a museum, and they have to stand in line with other tourists and locals. Cultural differences become very evident in these close spaces. How people talk, interact, and use space while moving in crowded and tight places differs greatly across cultures. Not everyone shares the same concept of interpersonal space, and while some are unphased when they bump into other people, others may be terribly offended. In countries with large populations and high density, people are often used to living in crowded cities and can appear oblivious to the bumping and jostling of a subway or public bus. American students who have not lived in big cities are often uncomfortable in these situations.

> Once, during a trip to Paris (in the summer), the Louvre was very crowded with tourists from all over the world, and some of our students felt uncomfortable moving through the crowd and seeing the exhibits. Seeing the 'Mona Lisa,' which was the most popular exhibit at the museum and very crowded, was a huge challenge. While other tourists did not hesitate to openly push others out of the way to move closer, some of our students stayed away from the crowds and only caught a glimpse of the painting from afar.

The most popular tourist sites attract a lot of visitors, both native and foreign, and students have to be advised about how to deal with crowds. How to move around while remaining with the group, keeping an eye on their possessions, not getting too friendly with other tourists, or posing for pictures with people they don't know are all topics you should cover. Students sometimes don't seem to have a "gut feeling" about what is okay and what is not, so you will need to help provide perspective.

> Students have to be told to be careful about their belongings in crowded spaces. On the trip to Goa, India, we decided to go to a beach restaurant for dinner. We were told to leave our shoes outside as they did not want sand inside the restaurant. After a hearty meal, when we came out, we couldn't find any of our footwear outside as someone had stolen them. We had to walk barefoot back to the hotel. Luckily, everyone had been wearing flip flops, and our hotel was on the beach and not very far. Yes, we lost our belongings, but we all had a good laugh about the situation. Don't expect THAT reaction very often.

The crowds you may encounter can be impressive. You will want to advise your students to be cognizant of their fellow group members at all times and try not to get separated. If you know you are headed to an area where there will be significant crowds and confusion, we suggest you point out a designated meeting place and time ahead of time and make sure the students know/see where that is before you begin exploring the site. That way, even if they do become separated, they will know where to find you and when.

Interacting with other visitors/tourists and locals alike can be one of the highlights of any international trip. But you will want to mention to your students that it is not a good idea to provide too much personal information or access to people they just met. The majority of people they encounter will be exploring the world and seeing new sites, just like them, but as we know there are also those out there looking to take advantage of unsuspecting travelers. So, it is best for students not to share their last names, hotel information, phone numbers, etc. with people too casually.

BECOMING COMFORTABLE...BUT NOT TOO COMFORTABLE

Despite all your good intentions and instruction in class, there will be instances that arise that you did not discuss but for which the group may need to have a sense of how to handle the situation. For example, it never occurred to us before the first trip to India to talk to the students about taking pictures with strangers until we saw it happen.

Unfortunately, there are some people who will make ill use of a student's image or photo. Students should refrain from posing for photos with people they don't know or, if possible, permitting people to take pictures of them (other than accidental inclusion in someone else's shot). We have noticed time and time again that some of our most attractive students (both male and female) will be approached by strangers for a photo. Particularly for the women, this can begin to feel uncomfortable as they end up posing for extended periods of time, while groups of men leer at them all, while one supposedly takes a picture. This can be particularly problematic, depending on how the students are dressed. Not only does the process of standing together for the photo create a great opportunity for pick pocketing or inappropriate touching—in the digital age, you really have no idea what that person is going to do with your photo. Of course, there are many times when the request for a photo is completely harmless (like when you visit a rural area and children are interested in taking a picture with a foreigner), but you should keep an eye out for this phenomenon and remind/help your students to use discretion.

In many countries, you will find "professional" photographers at common tourist sites who will take your picture, even as you pose for your own camera, without your permission and then try to sell you these pictures. You have to be careful with these photographers. A good idea is to ask your tour guide to select an appropriate photographer, who will accompany you through the site and take good pictures of each individual as well as the group. These photographers often know the best places to take the photos and will get great pictures of the group. With your guide, negotiate a price as a group and this will eliminate the need for each student to determine if they want this service or by whom. This also eliminates the need for everyone to get out their wallets, haggle a price, or make big purchases near a tourist site where someone might be watching just to evaluate them as a possible target. Additionally, the selection of a particular photographer will prevent the other vendors in the area who are also trying to sell you this service from hounding your group (or a particularly pretty young woman in the group) throughout the entire site.

Undoubtedly, you will also encounter vendors selling souvenirs and local crafts. This phenomenon is universal and the more famous the site you are visiting, the more vendors you will find. Advise the students to be careful of such vendors as they often show you a few items out on the street in order to attract you to another location where they have a store or stall (Note this is a great way for your group to become separated). In our experience, the uninitiated often end up paying inflated prices when out of earshot of competing merchants. This technique works best when the shopper is alone, so simply tell your students if they are interested in going into a particular souvenir shop, they should let you know and take several people with them. If you have a good guide, they can lead you to an honest store/vendor or help you bargain in general. On the other hand, sometimes your city guide will also try to lead you to restaurants or souvenir shops that pay him a commission for bringing customers. While sometimes you may get a good bargain at these places, there is also a chance that you may not. Make sure you discuss this with the tour company ahead of time and tell them you will not accept being taken to expensive shops or restaurants simply because the guide gets a commission. Also, do not hesitate to question the guide if you think this is happening and make sure students understand these issues. Trust us, we have seen plenty of tears shed when students feel they been taken by some souvenir salesperson.

It is best to have allotted time for shopping. Take students to shopping areas as a group and help them shop and find bargains. Trust us, they will want to do this but may be hesitant to shop/negotiate by themselves. If you do not know the best areas to shop, check out some travel websites, speak with friends and colleagues who have previously visited the country, and speak with your guide or tour company. Expect that there will be some places with traditional gift shops where it is easy to use credit cards but there may also be open-air shopping areas where things may be cheaper but require cash. Your students will most likely want to shop at both. Be aware that many of your students will love to shop and will wander from shop to shop, vendor to vendor, street to street in search of that next purchase. Make sure you are clear about where they are permitted to go and shop as well as how long they have to do so, so no one gets lost or causes a delay for the rest of the group. It is a good idea to let the students explore on their own, but you will need to balance that with safety issues and keeping to the schedule. You have to make sure that they understand the responsibility of keeping track of time and not delaying the group.

A good time to let the students explore on their own is at meal times. As you planned the itinerary, you should have considered where you might end up around meal times. You may want to make sure you break for meals in a central area where there are multiple restaurant options. If you are near a major tourist site at lunch time you are likely to find multiple eating options, hopefully at affordable prices, but they are going to be busy! Downtowns with fast food options are always a good idea, as they are affordable, and you are on a strict timetable. If restaurant options are limited, try to take students to a multi-cuisine restaurant, where they can find multiple options. Undoubtedly, though, affordability and time will be a major factor in choosing restaurants—at least for any meals that fall in the middle of a day's activities. When you let students go off on their own to find something to eat, let them know how much time they have before the next activity, where to meet you, and whether they would be better off at a fast food restaurant. Some students would prefer to sit and have a leisurely meal, and in some cultures, that can mean significantly more time than you may think. If you have a local guide, they may be able to make reservations and explain to the restaurant/servers your time constraints.

> We found the timing of meals particularly problematic in Europe. In Germany and France, it would not be uncommon for there to be a 5- to 10-minute wait after being seated for anyone to take an order, a 20-plus-minute wait for the food to arrive, and easily another 20–30-minute wait before the waitstaff returned to ask if anything else was needed or to bring the check. Most restaurants were much more focused on creating a space to enjoy the meal (more so than they are in many places in the U.S.). Not only did we come to realize how much Americans speed through our meals, but it was also frustrating at times when there were time pressures and the need to move along to the next item on the itinerary.

Some students (who have traveled frequently and internationally) can become overconfident and immediately feel comfortable in a new country. They adapt well and feel they know what to do. This may encourage the novice travelers to assume they, too, know what they are doing. This artificial comfort can sometimes make students careless and they will venture into areas which, at times, may put them or the group in danger. Whether it be taking an unnecessary risk like crossing a major highway to buy something or leaving the hotel for a nearby market place without informing the faculty, you should advise students explicitly against assuming they are "home" and have permission to go wherever and whenever they choose. You want student to embrace your host country, just make sure that they check with you before any adventure.

THE ROLE OF THE GUIDE

Your guide, if you should have one is an important factor for the success of the trip. If you hire a tour company, they are likely to arrange for a 24-hour escort as well as a local guide in every city. If you make arrangements yourself, you might have to hire a guide or a docent to take you through the sites, monuments, and museums. Either way, your students will have to realize that these guides are really just additional instructors. Many times students will be in a hurry to move on or explore and not appropriately listen to the narration of the guide.

When this happens, not only will they miss out on valuable information if they do this, it is also incredibly rude. You have to make sure that the students know what the expected behavioral norm is on this point. The guides/docents work very hard to provide interesting information to share about a site and in some places, you will find the guides have studied and received specialized training to be able to provide this service. This is a class, so students should be courteous and respectful and listen. They should treat this person like a visiting instructor in one of your classes.

You, however, should feel free to make allowances, if needed, such as at the end of the day when students may be tired. This might be the time for you to intervene and explain to the guide that the students are exhausted, and you need an abbreviated presentation. A good guide is adaptable, reads the group they are dealing with, and responds accordingly. They should also be well prepared, and entertaining. Guides can add a lot to the trip when they know their material and understand their audience, so hopefully you did your research and selected a good guide.

TRAVELING BETWEEN CITIES

Traveling within the country, the students get to experience more of the day-to-day aspect of life in that country and also understand the differences in the landscape and the culture. Traveling between cities can also be a challenge and may require a lot of patience and resilience from the students. The environment and culture can vary significantly as you travel within a country. Life in smaller cities is different than in the larger metropolitan areas and the customs, expectations and standards for acceptable clothing, behavior, can vary by location, region, degree of urbanization etc. For instance, your students will likely draw little attention in large, cosmopolitan cities where people are used to foreign tourists. On the other hand, in smaller cities or rural areas where there are fewer tourists, your group will be highly noticeable and there may be less understanding (or tolerance) of differences in attire or behavior. For example, while most Mexican women would not go out in public in shorts and a camisole even on the hottest day, your students will draw less attention in Mexico City if they were to do so then they would in rural areas like Oaxaca. The students have to be reminded to be aware of that and adapt their behavior and understanding to the environment. Additionally, smaller cities or rural areas may be less developed than your students expect. This can lead to some interesting challenges and you will want the group to be flexible. Whether it be no restaurants (outside the hotel) being open past dark or the lack of cell phone signal, we guarantee if you take your students outside of major metropolitan areas you will bump into some unexpected aspect of not being "home." You want to facilitate your students learning and to do that they need to be prepared and open to the experience. So, while you may have discussed this in class, make sure to remind/prepare students as you move to these rural areas that things may operate very differently. In the long run, these are valuable experiences, make for a great learning experience and also provide some of the most vivid memories the students take from the trip.

> Once, on a trip to a rural mountain village in South Asia, we arrived to find that our hotel (and most of the village) had no electricity due to a bus hitting a single electrical pole. Ordinarily, this would not have been much of an issue, but our hotel was built into the side of the mountain. While each room had huge picture windows with extraordinary views, the hallways were on the inside and completely dark without electricity. The hotel supplied us with candles, which we had to use to get to our rooms and, later that night, in our rooms to see. As the day went on, the students could not charge their phones, and there was no hot water, etc. Even though we were staying at the nicest hotel in town, the living conditions were far from what was expected. Nevertheless, because the students understood the rural nature of where we were, they were not too bothered and had fun finding their rooms and belongings in the candlelight. Some would later say they appreciated the "ambience" of the hotel.

DON'T BE AFRAID TO ASK

Imagine if a visitor to your city asked you for recommendations for a restaurant, where to find a certain kind of store, or even directions, you would be happy to help. People around the world are generally proud of their home town and country and extremely helpful. Don't be afraid to ask the people you meet for recommendations and explain that your group is there to learn. This rule applies not only to the people you meet but also to the hotel staff and guides you use.

Minor health issues are a common occurrence, but when they happen so far from home, they might require medical attention. Expect that your students will come to you for help with even the most minor of health issues such as a rash or blister. On the one hand, that is good because you would rather know about an issue before it gets worse, but it also means that you need to be ready for a variety of issues. As we discussed in the pre-departure chapter, you should have an emergency plan that will provide guidance in accordance with your institution's policies. However, if your emergency plan does not cover minor issues, ask the hotel for advice. Good hotels often have doctors on staff (some better than others) but even if they don't ask the hotel for assistance before you go out on your own to find a doctor or a pharmacy. Not only will they know where the closest pharmacy or medical provider is, but they will also often provide transportation or pick up basic medical supplies for you. In case of major issues that might require hospitalization, you can again turn to your hotel for assistance. They know and often have existing relationships with the local hospitals and doctors and may be able to assist with logistics of seeking major medical attention. While your emergency plan should lay out the procedures for you to follow, once on-site, it's good to consult with the hotel or tour agent about hospitals and pharmacies, should you need these services.

Don't be afraid to ask your tour guides and hotel about other services as well. On our trips to India, we found that students love to buy sarees. We usually take students to a saree shop, but then they need their blouses for the saree tailored. We have learned to inquire with our hotel, and they often can arrange for a tailor to come and take the orders and deliver the blouses back to the hotel the next day. We have also utilized the assistance of our hotels and guides to arrange a henna artist to come to the hotel (students love to get henna done on their hands and feet) as well as to have a Holi (Indian festival of colors) celebration on the beach in Goa, so the students could get an idea of a cultural festival. While in Germany on July 4th, we put together an impromptu barbecue with the assistance of our guides for the students to celebrate Independence Day. We were surprised to discover how challenging it was to explain (and then find) some of the traditional 4th of July food staples we all took for granted. When the students first encountered what the staff had purchased as "hot dogs," there was a long pause followed by significant good-natured laughter. This resulted in a long discussion among the students and staff about how and why Americans celebrated their Independence Day. Working with the hotel, guides, and local citizenry can not only facilitate your activities but can also make them much more memorable.

GOING HOME

It is time to go home. Make sure you double check the flight departure times and plan to get to the airport early to allow for check in, customs, and immigration. International airports are always very busy, and international departures and check-ins take much longer than those for domestic flights. Few countries process these flights as quickly as in the U.S., so give yourself plenty of time. How early you need to arrive at the airport will vary by location so

ON GROUND

make sure to ask at your hotel and your guide but three to four hours before your scheduled departure would not be unreasonable. Make sure that the bus or transportation you take to the airport is booked well ahead of time and knows the time of your departure. Local transportation people should be able to advise you on how much time it will take to get to the airport and check in, but if you are the slightest bit unsure, request to go early. Don't forget, weather conditions and other unforeseen circumstances might also cause unnecessary delays. Once while leaving India, there was a significant thunder storm and a large tree fell in front of our hotel, blocking the road. It delayed the journey to the airport by almost an hour and a half. Since we prepared the students to leave early, we made it on time (after watching people in the neighborhood arrive with axes and saws to remove the tree and clear the drive). It is better to arrive at the airport many hours before a flight than to miss a flight because you were late.

> We had one colleague who, upon the suggestion of a local guide, headed to the airport less than one hour before their flight. What apparently had been lost in translation was that while the group's first flight was domestic, they were transferring to an international flight to return home and did not have enough time to do so. Well, the group missed their international flight, and due to booking challenges, it took multiple days to get the entire group home and cost the university thousands of dollars in rebooking fees, and the group was unable to travel together, so some members got home days before others (and without their faculty member).

As you consider what time to leave for the airport, you will also want to consider the time it will take for your group to check out of the hotel. We strongly recommend you have your students pack as much as they can <u>and weigh their bags</u> the night before you leave. This way if they have to move things across cases (or get other students to carry things for them) to avoid over-weight baggage fees, it can all be settled long before the group is trying to leave. They will also have to pay any room charges they may have incurred. Checkout has to be done individually and as everyone is doing this at the same time, this can easily overwhelm the front desk. So, tell the students to settle their accounts ahead of time. Finally, make sure that each student double checks their rooms and bags to ensure they did not leave anything of value behind—especially their passports! All of this can take an amazingly long amount of time, so build it into your schedule.

ON GROUND

Once you are all ready and, in the lobby, it is time to load the bus. Many hotels request that the students leave their bags outside their rooms and an attendant will deliver the bags to the lobby. This is a convenient service but requires some advance time. Everyone will have to identify their bags in the lobby one last time before they are loaded on the bus to the airport. Between settling accounts and identifying bags, we suggest you inquire with the hotel about the checkout procedures ahead of time so that you can allot the appropriate amount of time in your schedule.

Once at the airport, it is important for each student to take possession of all their own bags and immediately begin the check-in process. Usually, each passenger will have to check individually, even if you are on a group ticket. Just as you did upon arrival, we suggest you have one faculty member at the beginning of the line and one at the end. You will want to be there to make sure all the students are checked in, bags are within the weight limit (or excess fees are paid, which, in some airports, requires that you leave the line, go to a different station to pay, and then return to the end of the line), and students all have boarding passes. Then make sure that everyone gets through security without any problems. In some countries, this includes a stop at immigration and even payment of an "exit fee." Make sure everyone has the exit fee money and has cash as many places will not accept credit cards for this payment. Some students may be just about out of money by this time. Finally, you want to make sure your entire group has passed through all these steps, everyone knows where your gate is, and when they need to be at the gate to meet you **before** you permit any individual time for them to purchase food or last-minute souvenirs in the airport. Students will often be in a hurry to run to some shop in the airport, but you want to be sure you do not lose anyone before your group boards the flight home.

> **By this point in the trip the students have become accustomed to counting on you for almost everything. Make sure they know (and have written down) all the information about their flights and flight numbers. That way if they get separated from you in the airport, they can at least find their way to the appropriate gate. You might be shocked by the number of times we discover that our students have no idea what airline or which flights they are supposed to be on. They just assume the faculty will be there to get them wherever they need to be.**

You got them all safely back on the flight home, so you may think you can relax. But you are not quite done. Remember your responsibility does not end at your home airport. We suggest that faculty use the time on the flight (or immediately on return) to make notes about any incidents which may have occurred on the trip or activities and places visited that worked well with their curriculum, and even vendors to use again (or not), so they can remember that for next time. An important aspect of your on-ground responsibility is to make sure you have notes on everything you might need to complete your paperwork on return. So, consider using this time and that daily notebook we discussed earlier to consolidate your materials.

Once they board the flight home, you will notice a change in your students. The closer to home they get, the less they think they need you or your instructions. Be clear with your students that they are not dismissed until everyone is back at your home airport and has collected their bags. If you have stops or layovers along the way, make sure you follow the trip protocol. Everyone should wait for the entire group and your instructions when they deplane. Make sure everyone knows the flight number, gate, and boarding/departure time for the next flight before they are dismissed to wander through the airport. Set a time 10–15 minutes before boarding for everyone to meet at the gate. You don't want to be in the situation of some of your students being on the flight while you are stuck waiting for a wayward straggler. These instructions are particularly important if your layover is in the U.S. Your students are now experienced world travelers and they will definitely think they can handle changing planes without your or the group's assistance. Trust us, they will wander off and come way too close to missing the flight because they "knew what they were doing."

> We once had half a dozen students who went to a Chili's in the **DFW** airport that was right across from the gate (because they just **HAD** to have American food and couldn't wait until after the final 45-minute leg of our journey was completed to eat) and they did not notice that their flight was boarding. They had not been checking their phones and we had to go looking for them. Once found, it took time to get them all to the gate as they had not received their food but had consumed soft drinks. They had to settle their checks, get their food to go, and hurry to the gate. Needless to say, the experience was stressful for the entire group who were waiting to board.

Once you land at home, tell the students they are not to leave the airport after collecting their bags **before** checking out with you. You will need to have a sense that everyone has found all their bags and has a ride home. You can't go home yourself until you confirm this as if there is a lost bag the student will probably want your assistance filing the paperwork. While all this sounds a little like overkill, remember you are the one responsible for what happens to the students until the trip is finished; and it's not finished until you hand them off to whoever is picking them up or they have found their ride (personal car, taxi, bus, etc.) home.

CONCLUSION

Being in a new country on a course-based trip can be stressful and also challenging at times, but the more efficiently your travel is organized, managed, and implemented, the more enjoyable and memorable the trip is for both you and your students. What matters in the end is the student learning experience and what the students take away from the trip. We as faculty have learned a little more from each trip about how to handle the challenges and what to do or not to do, while in a new country. You may or may not encounter other experiences that are similar to those discussed, but we hope that these experiences provide a good place to start for guidance on the questions that you and your students might have while traveling.

CHECKLIST

- ☐ As soon as you land
- ☐ Hotel check-in
- ☐ Commitment to the itinerary
- ☐ Evening briefing
- ☐ Group dynamics
- ☐ Cultural understanding and expectations on ground
- ☐ Role of the guide
- ☐ Traveling between cities
- ☐ Medical issues
- ☐ Safety
- ☐ Don't be afraid to ask
- ☐ Going home

REFERENCE

World Customs Organization. 2018. "Recommendation of the Customs Co-Operation Council for a Simplified Customs Control, Based on the Dual-Channel System, of Passengers Arriving by Air." www.wcoomd.org/en/about-us/legal-instruments/recommendations/pf_recommendations/pfrecomm312passengersarriveair.aspx (Accessed September 13, 2018).

Chapter Nine
How Far Is Too Far?

International travel is not always the easy and enlightening experience we might hope for. For some students such travel can push the boundaries of their cultural, religious, or political comfort zone. In this chapter, we discuss the challenges that even the most modest international experience may pose for students and discuss ways to accommodate and/or prevent these issues.

Let's be honest, not every student is as emotionally, psychologically, or culturally ready for international travel as you might hope. International travel can represent a disruption of their relationships, unsettle their understanding of how the world works and looks, and cause them to question their place in the world. The exposure to new cultures, peoples, ideas, and conditions can be overwhelming at times, and the open-minded enthusiasm with which students may have started can dwindle with exhaustion. Learning becomes difficult when students are not open to new information. Therefore, it is important for you to recognize the factors which may influence the ability of your students to process information and ideas.

Just how far can you take students from their comfort zone? How far is too far? The answer in part depends on how well you prepare the students for the experience (which we cover in Chapter Three) and in part on the structure you provide in the travel and your availability to them while on ground (which we cover in Chapter Eight). If the students know what to expect and have an understanding of the differences, then they will have had time to do some self-reflection to prepare themselves for those differences. They will spend more time on absorbing the experiences rather than on trying to make sense of unfamiliar ideas and adjusting their perspective. Regardless of how well they have been prepared, though, the trip may be overwhelming. In this chapter, we want to discuss what are common reactions to the new cultures and experiences encountered during study abroad (i.e., culture shock), what you can expect, how to help students deal with them, and how to manage the additional strain of students who are struggling to adapt to their international experience.

While traveling with students you have to be prepared for anything. And by anything, we mean <u>anything</u>. For instance, students will knock on your hotel room at 2:00 a.m. in the morning, because they are upset about something or do not feel well, and you have to be prepared to rush out in your pajamas (did we mention that you should remember to take a dressing gown/pajamas or sleep in appropriate clothes, so that you can be ready to go at 2:00 a.m. in the morning?). This is your class and you are their teacher at all times, but there might be times when they need you to be their friend and confidante. However, you should make sure you enjoy the trip as well. Don't be afraid to ask your colleagues to share student responsibility. That way one faculty is not on 24-hour duty. How to balance these demands and roles (and get some sleep!) is different for every trip. What demands are placed on faculty members may be determined by the role the students "assign" to faculty, so you need to be prepared to shift responsibilities. If one faculty member is taken into the students' confidence for personal issues and is up all night talking, other faculty members need to be prepared to lead the group while giving that faculty member a break for a nap or just a little free time to relax. While you should always stay on top of the mood of the students and their group dynamic, you need to communicate with your colleagues to make sure you are managing the time, travel, and stressors of the trip on yourselves as well. Be willing to take on more responsibility if one of your colleagues needs a break. Leading a group of students can take its toll on even the strongest of us, so step up so that the trip continues smoothly. It is amazing what a little quiet time or a nap can accomplish.

EXPECTATIONS OF ADJUSTING TO STUDY ABROAD

Expect your students to undergo a fairly typical adjustment cycle during the first few days of your stay. This cross-cultural adjustment cycle has several stages that manifest themselves through a variety of inward and outward "symptoms." The stages can be termed initial euphoria, irritation/hostility, initial adjustment, gradual adjustment, and adaptation/biculturalism. There is also a reverse culture shock that occurs when students return home. Think of it like a roller coaster. Both faculty and students need to recognize that virtually every student will have days where they hate the destination as well as days where they love the destination. This up and down cycle is normal and natural as students adjust to a new culture (Brein and David 1971; Pedersen 1995).

The emotional roller coaster is partly due to the excitement built up over the course and partly due to the travel itself, which often takes the students out of their comfort zone. The farther the destination is, the more likely students will step off the plane tired, hungry, and feeling in need of a shower—generally, not ready to learn. They are also likely to feel a bit shy and anxious as well, wondering

HOW FAR IS TOO FAR?

what they have gotten themselves into. However, they will usually rally quickly as they start to explore the destination and their enthusiasm returns.

Once the novelty wears off, though, students begin to feel the effects of being outside their comfort zone. Everything and everyone becomes frustrating as they try to adapt to their new environment. Loneliness, disappointment, depression, homesickness, and irritability are common for many students until they adjust to the destination. Once they have become accustomed to the locale, students accept what was at first frustrating and embrace their study abroad experience. Not all students progress through all of the stages, with some stagnating at the mental isolation stage.

One might say the reason we engage in study abroad is to force us to examine how we see the world. Whether your students even consider this a reason for travel, the fact is they (and you) WILL run into situations that are different, uncomfortable, and may challenge worldviews. Since your time on ground is limited you need to help students recognize when these challenges occur and provide the tools to process the new information and experiences.

FACULTY NEED TO MODEL BEHAVIOR

Faculty can go a long way toward easing the discomfort of being far from home by demonstrating the proper attitude, respect, and excitement for the experiences everyone will share during the trip. You need to model the appropriate behavior. For example, in Korea people will focus their complete attention on the most important person first and will complete their interaction with someone they are already engaged with before they even acknowledge a person who has just arrived. Don't be impatient and try to force your way into a discussion unless specifically invited to do so. You need to be prepared for these types of cultural differences and show respect for those differences by following the customs without complaint. Be the model and be prepared to help the students understand the behavior. The further away students are from their comfort zone, the more they are going to have to process. While they will discuss the day with roommates and classmates on an on-going basis, when they are overwhelmed or simply unsure how to process what they are seeing or doing, the students lean heavily on the faculty. In those cases, we not only have to lead by example, but we HAVE to be there for them by helping them understand either by discussing questions they have or listening to them as they work to process something outside of their norm.

Faculty should do more than just model how to treat people, places, and things. You must ALSO model the excitement for learning and an openness to new ideas. Lead by example. Once on a trip to Mexico, our host served a traditional delicacy of fried crickets with guacamole. Taken aback, the students turned to the faculty member. While not thrilled about the prospect of eating insects, we smiled, giggled, and gave it a try. Showing the students it was okay to be uncertain but important to be open and polite taught a valuable lesson about dealing with new cultural experiences. And by the way, if you put enough guacamole on it you won't even notice the crickets!

If you are not excited, or at least interested, your students will quickly lose interest as they take their cue on the importance of an idea, activity, or view from you. You are the expert and if you are not interested, why should the students be? Even if the moment does not involve anything of great import to you, it may be something that a student is discovering for the first time. If you show indifference, boredom, or outright contempt, the student may miss out on a once-in-a-lifetime experience. This may mean you need to get out of your own comfort zone, though, and "be the adult." As such, we have eaten fried *gusanos* (worms) and crickets in Monterrey, Mexico, sang karaoke in South Korea, and tried Feni in Goa, with our students. Faculty showing just that little bit of adventurousness led the way for the group to embrace the host country. The lack of interest, however, can have the opposite effect. So, be engaged (even if you do not want to be).

CHALLENGES

Regardless of how many times you tell and show students they will be stepping into a different culture with different norms, they will still take time to adjust to the differences. While we can't possibly cover everything you might encounter here, we will address some common challenges.

Unrealistic Expectations

Students may expect everything to be exotic, exciting, breathtaking, or awesome. The Louvre or Windsor Castle rarely disappoint, but after 10 castles, churches, or monasteries, the wow factor wears off and students lose their sense of wonder (particularly if their feet hurt, it is 105 degrees, or it is raining and cold). Students approach their travel experience as if everything will be magical and perfect and when it isn't they become disenchanted and begin to question why they are there and if the entire trip will be a disappointment.

> On our first trip to London, we did a nighttime "Jack the Ripper" tour, where you walk from one attack sight to the next and the tour guide discusses the theories and evidence. It is a very popular tourist attraction. However, the night we did the tour was unusually cold, so we

> spent the entire two plus hours shaking and paid little attention to the guide. What we thought would be a "cool" experience learning about the still unsolved Jack the Ripper murders did not quite meet our expectations as we were all too distracted by the temperature.

Home Sickness

Missing home may surprise some students and be a personal disappointment. They may feel they are adults and should be mature enough to be away and on their own for a few days to a few weeks. And yet, they often miss friends, family, and even just the familiarity of home. This disrupts their ability to experience and learn from the travel. They are either thinking of what they are missing back home and not tuning into what is around them or they are embarrassed that they can't handle being away from home and isolate themselves and don't get any experiential knowledge.

Even if they are not homesick, without exception you will find students miss food from home. Even if they end up loving callaloo or paella, many students eventually seek out a McDonald's or other American fast food comfort food. For some it is the food and for others the exhaustion of knowing what to order that is too much and they will seek out something familiar. When they do, they often find even familiar food is not the same. No matter where they travel, there is always going to be something they will miss that they simply can't get in other countries. This has a similar effect to general homesickness, making students think more about what they are possibly missing back home and actually missing what is going on right around them.

Need to Be Self-Reliant

Another common issue for course-based study abroad students is the need for self-reliance. While they are traveling with a group and many logistics are likely taken care of for them, students still have to manage their personal budget, wash their clothes, and be on time for each day's schedule. For some, this may be the first time they have really had to fend for themselves, so don't be surprised if they feel a bit uncertain or if you have to provide guidance. The need to be responsible for their own basic needs can be an overwhelming feeling that the student wonders if they will ever overcome.

Poverty

Exposure to any level of poverty may be particularly shocking to students, yet the differences in economic conditions may be more visible to our students when they travel. As outsiders observing everything with fresh eyes, it is common for students to see things for the first time that may exist in their own community but were invisible to them. While there are people begging and animals scrounging for scraps, students notice the locals may be carrying on with their day with little recognition of the less fortunate. This is when many students will be shocked to realize they do the same in their own culture.

Gender Roles

Society does not treat men and women equally and your female students may experience the world in a much different way than their male classmates. You should expect your female students to be surprised by the personal health and safety concerns as well as differences in gender identities, roles, and norms. They may well be treated differently or be expected to treat others differently. Their behavior, while being common in the U.S., may be viewed differently, and negatively, abroad. Use this as a teaching moment for both the male and female students. We suggest you discuss and help your students consider their own views on gender in society. Remember, all aspects of international travel are learning opportunities, even when they are not necessarily the focus of your class.

Treatment of Children

Childhood is viewed in the U.S. as a time to play and learn. At the very least, we believe children should be in school. Yet, depending on your destination, children may be more likely to be seen working than at school depending on economic, social, or political factors. While your students may be shocked to see small children forced to work or possibly prohibited from going to school, understanding the reasons behind this perspective on the treatment of children before simply condemning it is essential. If you are traveling to a country where these conditions exist, you will need to discuss this with your students ahead of time.

HOW TO MAKE FAR AWAY LESS UNCOMFORTABLE

While some adjustment and uncertainty are to be expected, there are a number of things you can do to limit it. Explaining what to expect, providing pictures, descriptions, and examples (to make it real), while discussing different cultural dynamics in your class or pre-departure meetings is an important start. That said, knowing that something exists does not necessarily help students understand why it exists. Students can still view different standards and values as wrong instead of just different. To properly prepare students for such challenges to their world view, you must provide cultural explanations and history, so they will have tools to place into context the differences when they see them.

Have students set a goal for their study abroad experience before they travel. Whatever their study abroad goal is, periodically remind them why they are studying abroad during the trip so that when they are tired and out of sorts, they can refocus on something positive. Students will continually discuss their experiences as they happen. If one of the students is depressed about something they have seen, or the group is focused on something negative intentionally make them discuss the condition (such as poverty) in the U.S. so they don't get judgmental or simply remind the group of another aspect of your trip which everyone found funny to lighten the mood.

Personal Supports: Thinking and Feeling

Make students aware of the stages of cultural adjustment so that they can recognize their reactions for what they are: part of a natural process. Help students take stock of particular situations and how they react to them. Emphasize flexibility and tolerance and remind them that things will be different, and they should expect that things will be different. Also, help them to recognize that they will not understand everything immediately and that a sense of ambiguity or uncertainty is OK. Encourage patience and help them identify those things that are the biggest stressors as well as what helps them manage their stress. While they may not be able to avoid stressors, they can know when they will be encountering them and prepare to manage them.

Encourage students to think positively, to find humor in their experiences, and not take themselves too seriously; being confused or uncertain about something is OK. If they knew everything, they wouldn't need to go to school or travel abroad.

Social Supports

Faculty are generally more experienced travelers than students and often need to serve as escorts for language and safety support when doing things like shopping or navigating in or out of tourist attractions. Crowds and haggling can be overwhelming, particularly when vendors are aggressive. Faculty can be reassuring the further the students are from their comfort zone, so expect that students will gravitate toward you when they feel out of their element. We have often experienced that the students will want to hang with us even on their free time. Whether you want the role or not, you are a big part of their social support system; be there for them.

Course-based study abroad is not a solitary endeavor. Students will have a group of classmates, faculty, and local guides to rely on. Remind students early on to identify sources of support and the types of support that each can best offer, so if they need a little extra support, they know where to get it. If you have created a positive group dynamic, if students are confused or troubled by something they have seen, they should feel comfortable asking you or the guide about it. If they need some quiet/downtime, they should be able to ask their classmates to consider this. And, while one reason to engage in study abroad is to experience the world and expand your horizons that doesn't mean you have to cut yourself off from your family and friends back home. Help students to plan in advance how they will keep in contact with their family and friends. Remind students not to isolate themselves! If they feel the need to talk to Mom, call her! As we stated at the beginning of the book, course-based study abroad is a learning <u>community</u>. Sharing their experiences (both good and bad) with their classmates and you can help students deal with the inevitable low points of travel and make these more bearable.

Get to Know the Locals

We have found that scheduling time to get to know the people of the country we are visiting creates a bond that can last long after the trip is a distant memory. Creating an opportunity to interact helps students get a better perspective of the country and culture, helping them delve into the country and not just view it as an outsider. Talking to and engaging with people who are not simply trying to sell you something gives you insight into how they view the world and you. This can open the door to a conversation where everyone learns about each other and eliminates pre-conceived, and quite possibly erroneous, notions of who you and they really are. You will find the distance between the students and the destination becomes shorter as they get to know the locals and they get to know you. Yes, there will be differences, but your students and you will also find you share many things, making them feel more "at home."

Creating a Supportive Atmosphere

From our very first trip with students, we have taken the approach that the students should develop a positive relationship among themselves. Students should have a chance to get to know each other in your preparation course or pre-departure sessions. Not only does this help limit personal conflicts as weariness, distance, heat, etc. take their toll, but also creates a sense of togetherness that serves as an additional means of group support. We continually stress the importance of being part of a group that travels, learns, and looks out for each other. We have all heard the stories of students who, being on their own, had harrowing experiences. A close-knit group will look out for each other more carefully than one where the students do not know each other well. So, you should aim at the very least to build a positive group dynamic before you travel—it will help provide a support structure and reduce the stress of the unknown if the students are already friends.

So, besides being in class with each other for a semester, how can you develop a positive supportive group? Going to a restaurant that serves food from your destination, if available, is a good way to build camaraderie. Sharing a meal is a universal human experience that creates a sense of community. Trying food together that many of you have perhaps not tasted before will reduce the insecurity that students may feel individually. It is a way of gaining a comfort level but also to share in an experience that will bring the group together. It provides a bonding experience where you can all begin to realize that your trip is not just an abstract thing in the future, but something you will all participate in together. Furthermore, if students are unsure how to act around faculty (we can be scary and seem distant because of our position of authority), they have an opportunity to become more comfortable with you in a social setting.

If there is a festival or cultural event related to the country you're visiting near your campus, take your students to it as a group. You can get a preview or a small taste of what you will be seeing on your trip. Not only will you be doing an activity together, but you can use it as a way to start a conversation among your students about your trip. Every opportunity to get your students to engage in the material related to your class trip together builds more of a cohesive group.

Physical Supports

While emotional support is important, everyone needs to be physically ready to travel. Before and throughout travel, encourage students to eat healthy, drink plenty of water, and get plenty of rest (well at least try to encourage them to sleep!). Look for any problem behaviors (e.g., excessive consumption of alcohol) that demonstrate nervousness and make plans with the student to manage them. Moderate exercise can be a strong counter to the cultural stress and fatigue that is common when you are far away from home. And don't forget to encourage students to think about bringing a few comfort food snacks.

> One of the author's comfort "foods" is Diet Coke. Allergies and a long bus ride resulted in queasiness, so our guide made a number of stops before he was able to find Diet Coke and the problem was solved. With each unsuccessful stop, the entire group found it more and more hilarious that, despite the "Coca Cola" signs on many of these shops, they only sold Pepsi. The next day and for the remaining week or so of the trip, the guide filled the cooler on the bus not only with cold water but with enough Diet Coke for the group. The Diet Coke Challenge not only became a fond memory for the group but also showed the importance of the comforts of home as well as the extraordinary kindness of our guide, Tombi.

HOW FAR IS TOO FAR?

While we have already addressed this in the planning chapter, we should remind you that providing a comfortable hotel so that students can retreat when they feel overwhelmed is worth the extra expense. While some faculty would argue that part of the study abroad experience is to not isolate yourself from the culture you are visiting, our advice is that sometimes students need the comfortable space. Use the quiet, comfortable, hopefully serene atmosphere of your hotel to create a safe space for students to relax. Sometimes, far away can be too far and a little comfort can close that distance a little, help them get a good night's sleep, and be refreshed to take on the new experiences the next day.

EMERGENCY BAG

We have taken to carrying what a colleague jokingly refers to as a Mary Poppins Bag. Based on the schedule for the day, the bag is filled with a wide variety of "emergency" items intended to help the group with any discomfort which may arise. The bag routinely includes ibuprofen/acetaminophen, bismuth tablets, antacids, Dramamine, Imodium, moleskin, antihistamines, and the basics of a first aid kit, bandages, antibiotic wipes, etc. In more remote and less developed destinations, the bag gets heavier with facial tissue, toilet paper, bug repellent, sunscreen, extra bottles of water, rehydration packets, a bandana/handkerchief, a hat, a hand fan, duct tape (in case a bag, someone's shoes, or anything else falls apart), an eye glass repair kit, and sanitary products for women. In our experience, students will not think about these things. Last, but certainly not least, are a cache of snacks for when travel is delayed, or someone's blood sugar dips, and they need a little pick me up. And before you bemoan the possibility of schlepping around a bag everywhere, know that we often leave it on the bus or van we are using for the day; it could also be left in a rental locker if you are going to remain in the same area for an extended time during the day or evening. Trust us, having these items on hand will reduce many an issue from becoming a problem and you will be glad you have it.

REVERSE CULTURE SHOCK

Students are often surprised to find it may take a while to readjust to life at home. An important part of the intercultural learning takes place after the study abroad experience when students see their own country or city through a new perspective. Re-evaluation of one's own country and culture is an important part of the process. Students will have to work to make meaning of a powerful experience.

It takes time to sort it all out, and there are often moments of great joy at seeing or experiencing something wonderous or sadness when experiencing something somber along the way. Give students the chance to share and process their experience with you and communicate to friends and family before leaving and upon return the need to listen and be supportive as well. Most students say that their experience studying abroad was "life-changing," and how that eventually manifests itself in their life may take them awhile to figure out.

International travel of any distance can be positive or negative—it depends on the level of preparation. Just be advised, the further you take students from what they know, the more work you have to put into preparation and support.

CHECKLIST

- ☐ Expectations of adjusting to study abroad
- ☐ Faculty need to model behavior
- ☐ Challenges
- ☐ Unrealistic expectations
- ☐ Home sickness
- ☐ Need to be self-reliant
- ☐ Poverty
- ☐ Gender roles
- ☐ Treatment of children
- ☐ How to make far away less uncomfortable
- ☐ Personal supports: thinking and feeling
- ☐ Social supports
- ☐ Get to know the locals
- ☐ Creating a supportive atmosphere
- ☐ Physical supports
- ☐ Emergency bag
- ☐ Reverse culture shock

REFERENCES

Brein, Micheal and Kenneth H. David. 1971. "Intercultural Communication and the Adjustment of the Sojourner." *Psychological Bulletin* 76: 215–230.

Pedersen, Paul. 1995. *The Five Stages of Culture Shock: Critical Incidents Around the World.* Westport, CT: Greenwood Press.

Chapter Ten

Is It Worth It?

If you are still reading our book, it means we have not overwhelmed or scared you to the point of giving up. Great! In this chapter, the authors offer some concluding remarks about the value of the study abroad experience—for the student, instructor, department, and institution. Course-based study abroad activities such as those discussed in this book are incredibly time consuming and can be challenging, but they can also be life-changing. The authors examine whether it is worth the time, effort, and expense.

THE DOWNSIDE

As you can tell, we think leading course-based study abroad experiences are not only important for the student; it is a significant endeavor for you, the instructor, as well. There are some serious downsides to doing this kind of work and we will be the first to admit it. It is incredibly time consuming. Hopefully, by this point, we have given you a sense of the months of preparation required, the hours of teaching, and the intensity of student interaction on the trip. If you are not that instructor who stays late in the evening working with student groups or other activities outside of your research, this is probably not your cup of tea. Undoubtedly, you are going to have to do virtually all of the work to make this happen. Some institutions will have more support and infrastructure than others to aid in your endeavor but don't be surprised if at minimum, you end up spending hours explaining to the different parts of campus what you are trying to do and why. Quite simply, the success of the entire endeavor is tied directly to your energy and efforts. And even after months of preparation, there is always a chance that the class or trip will not make. If you don't generate enough student interest, all your hours of work will be for naught.

The quality of your students' experience will also be determined by your commitment and engagement—especially once you are traveling. If you cannot imagine staying up late into the night talking with students or hearing their concerns, then you may not be the type of course leader needed. Not only are you going to be responsible for preparing and delivering the course content, but it will be up to you to make sure every aspect of the trip goes off without a hitch. A seamless travel experience is the foundation for students being able to truly absorb the course content through their on-ground experiences. That may mean you spend hours late at night negotiating roommate disputes, calling parents about concerning student behavior, mentoring students on cultural sensitivity or hotel etiquette, and even dealing with cases of unwanted sexual advances among your students. We have seen and had to deal with them all. If these issues arise, the role of faculty member can expand to include parent, counselor, and police officer.

You may even have issues with your colleagues. Every person has differing energy levels, endurance, and tempers. So, how the faculty leaders deal with the stress of traveling with students also varies. Some faculty who may be wonderful partners in planning and promoting a trip may disengage from students and issues when they become tired or may simply prefer not to deal with the issues which can arise in group dynamics. If this happens, you will be left to deal with all the issues that develop and the uncertainty among your students, hotel staff, and local providers that differing leadership styles create.

Finally, there are innumerable outside factors that can jeopardize your trip or overall experience. If one of your group is a victim of a crime or has a mental breakdown on the trip (been there, seen it!), if there is a transportation strike or interruption that makes it impossible to stay with your itinerary, if there is a hurricane or volcanic eruption which delays your return flights for days or weeks—your course-based study abroad experience can take a turn you never expected. When things go wrong, it is not just a case of your own inconvenience, remember you are going to be responsible for the safety, security, and educational experience of the entire group.

THE UPSIDE

But wait! Course-based study abroad is a powerful learning tool that is too valuable to discard simply because of the time, effort, and uncertainties involved. If you do a good job and provide a solid educational experience, the effect on your students will be amazing! You will create life-long traveler learners. They will embrace the course material in a deeper, more meaningful way than any in-class activity could ever provide. Learning-based travel will expand their horizons and make your students more aware of other cultures and perspectives—on all types of issues. It can be a life-changing experience for your students and they will become truly global citizens.

The benefits for your department and university can be significant as well. When students return to campus after a study abroad experience, they will bring with them stories, pictures, and a sense of excitement about course-based study abroad that will be infectious. Don't be surprised if very quickly after your return you start getting questions from other students about when and where you are going next. These trips do much to build departmental cohesion and a tone of collegiality and excitement for learning that extends beyond the classroom. They build deep relationships both among the students and between students and faculty/the department. You will find the shared memories of experiences like hiking the Great Wall of China or touring Windsor Castle will create in your students a lifelong affinity for your department and the university.

For faculty, course-based study abroad can open the world to you and give you the opportunity to see places and have experiences you otherwise would never have a chance to do. As we have said many times, it is not a vacation, but it is a wonderful opportunity to see the world. Preparing to teach a course-based study abroad class will inevitably expand your knowledge and understanding of the focus of the class as well as the nation, people, and culture of your destination. As you have experienced the travel-based learning alongside your students, you will likely gain a greater appreciation as well as new perspective on the material. Your students will also get to witness you learning more about the material during the travel experience right along with them, showing them the power of life-long learning. And if you are like most of us, you will return invigorated (tired but invigorated), and your teaching of the material will be forever enriched.

Perhaps more importantly, course-based study abroad also helps you build deep and lasting relationships with your students. Traveling with students gives you a chance to know them more fully and the shared experiences of traveling can create a bond that lasts long beyond graduation. As this one author sat writing this chapter, she received a text from a former course-based study abroad student, relaying their excitement in finishing their first year in a PhD program, and another from one confirming her attendance in that student's upcoming law school graduation. Watching the transformation in your students as they experience the world and the learning process in a completely new way is a privilege that is rewarding beyond measure. Seeing their passion for the academic content bloom in the light of new countries and cultures is exciting and we promise it will make you remember why it is that we teach! Let's not forget, course-based study abroad can also be fun! Whether it is dancing with students late into the night outside the Louvre on a beautiful summer evening, sharing a pretzel at Hitler's Eagle's Nest high atop a mountain in Germany, or teaching a student how to swim in Barbados, traveling with students builds teaching memories that will last a lifetime!

IS IT WORTH IT?

Finally, course-based study abroad can be a truly transformational experience for you and your students. You will never look at the world (or your students) the same way!

Go out and explore the world! And take your students with you!!!

You won't regret it.

Additional Resources

Anthes, Susan and Lawson Crowe. 1991. "The Collaborative Course: Innovative Teaching and Learning." *Community/Junior College Quarterly of Research and Practice* 15 (4): 369–379.

Benson, Angela, Scott Johnson, John Duncan, Olga Shinkarvea, Gail Taylor, and Tod Treat. 2008. "College Participation in Distance Learning for Career and Technical Education." *Community College Journal of Research and Practice* 32 (9): 665–687.

Berardo, Kate and Darla K. Deardorff. 2012. *Building Cultural Competence: Innovative Activities and Models*. Herndon, VA: Stylus Publishing.

Berdan, Stacie Nevadomski, Allan Goodman, and William Gertz. 2015. *A Parent Guide to Study Abroad*. New York: Institute of International Education.

Bevis, Brawner Teresa. 2014. *A History of Higher Education Exchange: China and America*. Philadelphia: Routledge Publishing.

Blumenthal, Peggy, Crauford Goodwin, and Ulrich Teichler. 1996. *Academic Mobility in a Changing World: Regional and Global Trends*. London: Jessica Kingsley Publishers.

Brenner, Faye. 2015. *Transforming Student Travel: A Resource Guide for Educators*. Lanham, MD: Rowman & Littlefield Publishers.

Brewer, Elizabeth and Kiran Cunningham, eds. 2010. *Integrating Study Abroad into the Curriculum: Theory and Practice Across the Disciplines*. 1st ed. Herndon, VA: Stylus Publishing.

Chernotsky, Harry I. and Heidi H. Hobbs. 2018. *Crossing Borders: International Studies for the 21st Century*. 3rd ed. Washington, DC: CQ Press.

Davidson, Cathy N. 2011. "Collaborative Learning for the Digital Age." *The Chronicle of Higher Education*, August 26. http://chronicle.com/article/Collaborative-Learning-for-the/128789/ (Accessed January 1, 2014).

Davis, Matthew. 2012. "How Collaborative Learning Leads to Student Success." *Edutopia*. www.edutopia.org/stw-collaborative-learning-college-prep (Accessed January 1, 2014).

ADDITIONAL RESOURCES

Donald, James. 2007. "Internationalisation, Diversity and the Humanities Curriculum: Cosmopolitanism and Multiculturalism Revisited." *Journal of Philosophy of Education* 41 (3): 289–308.

Dzakiria, Hisham. June 2008. "Students' Accounts of the Need for Continuous Support in a Distance Learning Program." *Open Learning* 23 (2): 103–111.

Forrester, Gillian, Gary Motteram, Gillian Parkinson, and Diane Slaouti. 2005. "Going the Distance. Students' Experiences of Induction to Distance Learning in Higher Education." *Journal of Further and Higher Education* 29 (4): 293–306.

Freed, Barbara F. 1995. *Second Language Acquisition in a Study Abroad Context*. Amsterdam: John Benjamins Publishing.

Gadbury-Amyot, Cynthia, Jacquelyn Fried, and Sheryl Ernest Syme. 2007. "Technology in Teaching and Online Distance Learning: Two Model Programs." *Access* 21 (7): 10–17.

Gerlich, Nicholas. 2005. "Faculty Perceptions of Distance Learning." *Distance Education Report*, 9 (17): 8.

Green, Madeleine F. and Robert Shoenberg. 2006. *Where Faculty Live: Internationalizing the Disciplines*. Washington, DC: American Council on Education.

Haigh, Martin J. 2002. "Internationalisation of the Curriculum: Designing Inclusive Education for a Small World." *Journal of Geography in Higher Education* 26 (1): 49–66.

Hernandez, Magnolia, Margaret Wiedenhoeft, and David Wick. 2014. *NAFSA's Guide to Education Abroad for Advisers and Administrators*. 4th ed. New York: NAFSA.

Hess, Daniel J. 1997. *Studying Abroad/Learning Abroad: An Abridged Edition of the Whole World Guide to Culture Learning*. Boston: Nicholas Brealey Publishing.

Hicks, David. 2003. "Thirty Years of Global Education: A Reminder of Key Principles and Precedents." *Educational Review* 55 (3): 265–275.

Hobert, Carl F. 2013. *Raising Global IQ: Preparing Our Students for a Shrinking Planet*. Boston: Beacon Press.

Hoffa, William and Stephen C. DePaul. 2010. *A History of U.S. Study Abroad: 1965-Present*. Carlisle, PA: Forum on Education Abroad.

Hornberg, Sabine. 2002. "Human Rights Education as an Integral Part of General Education." *International Review of Education* 48 (3–4): 187–198.

Huang, Futao, Martin Finkelstein, and Michele Rostan, eds. 2014. *The Internationalization of the Academy: Changes, Realities and Prospects*. New York: Springer.

Jackson, M.G. 2003. "Internationalising the University Curriculum." *Journal of Geography in Higher Education* 27 (3): 325–340.

Kreber, Carolin. 2009. "Different Perspectives on Internationalization in Higher Education." *New Directions for Teaching and Learning* 118: 1–14.

ADDITIONAL RESOURCES

Lantis, Jeffrey S. and Jessica DuPlaga. 2010. *Global Classroom: An Essential Guide to Study Abroad* (International Studies Intensives). New York: Routledge.

LaVallie, Connor and Sean O'Bryan. 2012. *The Study Abroad Truth: You Might Just Discover Yourself, What You Need to Know Before, During, and After Your Journey!* 2nd ed. Chicago: Ham n' Egg Publishing.

Letterman, Margaret R. and Kimberly B. Dugan. Spring 2004. "Team Teaching a Cross-Disciplinary Honors Course: Preparation and Development." *College Teaching* 52 (2): 76–79.

Lewin, Ross. 2009a. "Transforming the Study Abroad Experience into a Collective Priority." *Peer Review* 11 (4): 8–11.

Lewin, Ross. 2009b. *The Handbook of Practice and Research in Study Abroad: Higher Education and the Quest for Global Citizenship*. New York: Routledge.

Lorenzetti, Jennifer Patterson. 2008. "Internationalism, Cross-Border Higher Education and Distance Learning-Lessons for Presidents who Care Enough to Do What is Right." *Distance Education Report* 12 (11): 5–7.

Lutterman-Aguilar, Ann and Orval Gingerich. 2002. "Experiential Pedagogy for Study Abroad: Educating for Global Citizenship." *Frontiers: The Interdisciplinary Journal of Study Abroad* 8: 41–82.

McCallon, Melanie and Bill Holmes. 2010. *Faculty-Led 360: Guide to Successful Study Abroad*. Saint Joseph, MI: Agapy LLC.

McMurtrie, Beth. June 2007. "International Educators Discuss Foreign Recruitment and Study Abroad." *Chronicle of Higher Education* 53 (40): 33.

Merkx, Gilbert W. and Riall W. Nolan. 2015. *Internationalizing the Academy: Lessons of Leadership in Higher Education*. Cambridge, MA: Harvard Education Press.

Morey, Ann Intili. 2000. "Changing Higher Education Curricula for a Global and Multicultural World." *Higher Education in Europe* XXV (1): 25–39.

Murphy, Moira. 2007. "Experiences in the Internationalization of Education. Strategies to Promote Equality of Opportunity at Monterray Tech." *Higher Education* 53 (2): 167–208.

Ninnes, Peter and Meeri Hellsten, eds. 2005. *Internationalizing Higher Education: Critical Explorations of Pedagogy and Policy*. Hong Kong: Comparative Education Research Centre.

Oberle, Holly. 2013. *College Abroad*. Saint Joseph, MI: Agapy LLC.

Olson, Christa L., Madeleine F. Green, and Barbara A. Hill. 2005. *Building a Strategic Framework for Comprehensive Internationalization*. Washington, DC: American Council on Education.

Olson, Christa L., Madeleine F. Green, and Barbara A. Hill. 2006. *A Handbook for Advancing Comprehensive Internationalization: What Institutions Can Do and What Students Should Learn*. Washington, DC: American Council on Education.

ADDITIONAL RESOURCES

Pandit, Kavita. 2009. "Leading Internationalization." *Annals of the Association of American Geographers* 99 (4): 645–656.

Pike, Graham and David Selby. 1988. *Global Teacher, Global Learner.* London: Hodder Education.

Pike, Graham and David Selby. 1995. *Reconnecting: from National to Global Curriculum.* Godalming, Surrey: World Wildlife Fund UK.

Richert, Bailey. 2015. *#StudyAbroadBecause: 50+ Reasons to Complete a Semester Overseas.* Kindle Edition. Bailey Richert.

Roed, Jannie. 2007. "Internationalizing the Curriculum: What Does It Mean?" *International Journal of Therapy and Rehabilitation* 14 (9): 390.

Roholt, Ross VeLure and Colleen Fisher. 2013. "Expect the Unexpected: International Short-Term Study Course Pedagogies and Practices." *Journal of Social Work Education* 49: 48–65.

Roth, Michael S. 2014. *Beyond the University: Why Liberal Education Matters.* New Haven, CT: Yale University Press.

Rubin, Amy Magaro. 1995. "Notes on Exchanges." *Chronicle of Higher Education* 41 (39): 40.

Sarobol, Nopporn. 2012. "Implementing Cooperative Learning in English Language Classroom: Thai University Students' Perceptions." *International Journal of Interdisciplinary Social Sciences* 6 (10): 111–122.

Savicki, Victor. 2008. *Developing Intercultural Competence and Transformation: Theory, Research, and Application in International Education.* Herndon, VA: Stylus Publishing, LLC.

Savicki, Victor and Elizabeth Brewer, eds. 2015. *Assessing Study Abroad: Theory, Tools and Practice.* Herndon, VA: Stylus Publishing.

Shaw, Carolyn and David Mendeloff. 2006. "Connecting Students Internationally to Explore Post-Conflict Peacebuilding." Presented at the Annual International Studies Association Conference, San Diego.

Slimbach, Richard. 2010. *Becoming World Wise: A Guide to Global Learning.* Herndon, VA: Stylus Publishing Inc.

Stiasny, Mary and Tim Gore. 2014. *Going Global: Knowledge-Based Economies for 21st Century Nations.* Bingley, West Yorkshire, United Kingdom: Emerald Group Publishing Limited.

Storti, Craig. 2007. *The Art of Crossing Cultures.* 2nd ed. Yarmouth, ME: Intercultural Press.

Stow, Robert. March 2005. "Minimizing the Distance in Distance Learning." *Athletic Therapy Today* 10 (2): 57–59.

Svensson, Lennart and Monne Wihlborg. 2010. "Internationalising the Content of Higher Education: The Need for a Curriculum Perspective." *Higher Education* 60: 595–613.

Toyoshima, Mihoko. 2007. "International Strategies of Universities in England." *London Review of Education* 5 (3): 265–280.

Vainio-Mattila, Arja. 2009. "Internationalizing Curriculum: A New Kind of Education?" *New Directions for Teaching and Learning* 118 (Summer): 95–103.

Vande Berg, Michael R., Michael Paige, and Kris Hemming Lou, eds. 2012. *Student Learning Abroad: What Our Students Are Learning, What They're Not, and What We Can Do About It*. Herndon, VA: Stylus Publishing.

Williamson, Wendy. 2008. *Study Abroad 101*. 2nd ed. Saint Joseph, MI: Agapy LLC.

Yates, Lyn and Michael Young. 2010. "Globalisation, Knowledge and the Curriculum." *European Journal of Education* 45 (1): 4–10.

Younes, Maha, N. and Sylvia M. Asay. 2003. "The World as a Classroom: The Impact of International Study Experiences on College Students." *College Teaching* 51(4): 141–147.

Ziegenfuss, Donna Harp and Patricia Lawler. 2008. "Collaborative Course Design: Changing the Process, Acknowledging the Context, and Implications for Academic Development." *International Journal for Academic Development* 13 (3): 151–160.

Index

academic discipline 5, 9, 13, 15, 57
accidents 105
accommodations vii, 17, 21, 24–27, 28, 30, 33, 34, 37–44, 46, 47, 50–52, 54, 73, 74, 77, 78, 80, 83, 84, 86, 87, 90–92, 95, 104, 110–112, 126, 127, 129, 132, 139–143, 145, 155, 158
accounts; see responsibility, faculty
acculturation 60
advisor 31, 102
airlines/airfare 3, 25, 26, 31–33, 36, 37, 43, 44, 65, 73, 74–77, 81–83, 86, 87, 90, 92
airports 123, 141, 143; departures 141

baggage; see luggage
bank 32, 48, 106
behavior viii, ix, 15–19, 33, 60, 61, 64–67, 72, 102–104, 108, 109, 114, 115, 119, 121, 130, 132–134, 139, 148, 151, 156, 158; expectations 58, 61, 62, 64, 65–69, 72, 74, 84, 103–105, 108, 109, 115, 119, 133, 139, 145; student; alcohol ix, 92, 119, 154; attire 9, 61, 65, 68, 69, 115, 119, 134, 139; dress 61, 62, 68, 115, 133, 136; cultural insensitivity 4, 62, 66, 147, 152, 158; drugs 17, 66, 102; eating 67, 68, 81, 92, 137, 149, 154; group dynamics 6, 9, 15, 17, 18, 55, 63, 65–67, 77, 100–108, 132, 153–156; illegal 17, 119, 130; safety 118, 151, 152; sex 17, 66, 119, 158; violence 102
briefings 129, 130, 133, 145
budget v, xii, 12, 13, 24, 36, 41, 43, 73, 74, 76, 77, 80, 83, 85, 86, 90–93, 95, 96, 100, 110, 111, 150; faculty 73, 75, 83–86, 90, 110, 111; students 24, 43, 83, 91–95, 150; tips and gratuities 84

cash 22, 45, 47, 48, 52, 54, 84, 106, 114, 117, 118, 120, 124, 137, 143
cell phone 15, 32, 42, 43, 48–51, 54, 105, 108, 112, 114, 116, 117, 120, 135, 139, 140, 144
chaperone ix, x, 102, 105
check-in 15, 16, 25, 39, 76, 126, 129, 141, 143, 145
checklist 20, 53, 72, 95, 112, 120, 145, 156
class viii, 6, 9, 22, 23, 26–28, 30–32, 53, 56–60, 64–71
communication 22, 49, 50, 54, 127, 156
credit cards 22, 32, 45, 47, 48, 54, 79, 106, 114, 117, 118, 120, 124, 137, 143

167

INDEX

crisis management plan 52
culture xii, 2, 4, 6, 7, 9, 35, 46, 53, 56–58, 60, 61, 68, 70, 111, 113, 126, 134, 139, 146, 147, 149, 151, 153, 155, 156, 159, 162; acculturation 60; assimilation 60; sensitivity 4, 8, 10, 158
culture shock 2, 4, 6–8, 60, 111, 113, 146–155; emotional 35, 41, 103, 146, 147, 154; homesickness 7, 148, 150; reverse (reintegration) 32, 71, 111–113, 147, 155, 156
currency 9, 47, 93, 95, 124
curriculum xi, 1–12, 21, 74, 77
class/course-offerings 56–60
cultural expectations 60–63, 66–69; engagement ix, 6, 7, 15, 60, 88, 109, 153, 157; globalization of 88; internationalizing x, 7, 88; learning objectives xiii, 3–5, 9, 19, 28, 33, 56, 57, 59, 70–71, 88; philosophy 8, 10, 39, 162; transformational i, iii, x, 11, 13, 20, 54, 71, 159, 160,161, 163, 164
customs and immigration 23, 61, 64, 68, 84, 121–125, 139, 141, 145, 148; debrief 32; dollar 49, 93, 95,124

emergency 19, 32, 39, 49, 51–53, 89, 90, 104, 105, 115, 116, 119, 140, 141, 155, 156; injuries 17, 23, 133
evaluation 98, 111

faculty 3, 5–9, 11, 13, 15, 17, 25, 29–33, 35, 36, 44, 50, 57, 58, 65, 67, 71, 73, 87, 88, 97–113, 115, 119, 121, 126, 132, 143, 145, 147–149, 152, 154, 156, 158, 159, 162; approval 14, 98, 99, 112; expenses 24, 39, 48, 49, 73, 81, 106; student ratio 36, 86, 101, 102, 112, 113
financial responsibilities xii, 2, 3, 6, 21, 25, 26, 31, 33–37, 39, 41–45, 54, 74–95, 98, 99, 100, 104, 105, 106, 113, 132, 142; leader 15–20; costs vii, xii, 3, 25, 39, 41, 49, 51, 73, 74, 75, 77, 79, 80, 81, 83, 84, 86, 87, 88, 89, 90, 91, 92, 93, 94, 95, 96, 99, 100, 105, 106, 117, 127, 131
fees 19, 25, 37, 42, 74, 76, 82, 89–91, 93, 98–100, 105
food 24, 28, 42, 68, 81, 137, 138, 141, 144, 150, 154
Forum on Education Abroad 5, 19

group dynamics 7–9, 15, 40, 58, 63, 65, 67, 101, 109, 131–133, 145, 147, 151, 153, 158
group-boarding 25
guides vii, viii, xi, 3, 9, 37–40, 46, 47, 54, 65, 74, 84–86, 111, 126, 128, 132, 138–141, 152

health 51, 52, 81, 100, 103, 140
homesickness 7, 148, 150
hospital 18, 51, 52
hostel *see* accommodations
hotel *see* also accommodations: amenities 24, 41–43, 95; location 41–42; services 42–43

identities 151
illness 18, 103, 150, 156
immersion 1, 5, 23, 34, 54, 58, 60
instructor 12, 17, 18, 22, 23, 59, 61, 62, 68, 85, 99, 100, 111, 112, 118, 119, 138, 139, 157
insurance 18, 37, 51, 52, 73, 81, 82, 86, 95, 100, 104, 105, 112, 114, 116, 117, 120
intercultural x, xii, 1, 4, 5, 8, 10–12, 53, 54, 107, 113, 147, 155, 156, 164; competence x, 10, 1, 12, 161, 164; global 2; tolerance 1, 5, 7, 56, 139, 146, 152

168

INDEX

international x 13, 1, 2, 5 7, 10 13, 16, 19, 23, 26, 28, 30, 32 34, 36, 48, 49, 51 54, 58, 61 65, 69, 71, 74, 75, 81 85, 88, 89, 91, 94, 100 103, 105 108, 112, 113, 116, 117, 123, 124, 128, 135, 141, 142, 146, 151, 156, 161 165

itinerary vii, ix, 12, 8, 14, 16 18, 24 31, 34 38, 40, 41, 43 46, 58, 60, 61, 65, 74, 77, 79, 80, 83, 91 93, 98, 100, 101, 103, 104, 107 111, 115, 127 129, 133, 137, 138, 145, 158; commitment to 38, 127, 128, 145; destination 21 23, 26, 27, 34, 35, 48, 54, 98, 106, 112, 116, 122

learning viii x, 12, 13, 1 7, 9, 11, 12, 21 23, 27, 34, 53 57, 59, 60, 68, 70, 71, 88, 89, 100, 107, 114, 128, 130, 140, 145, 146, 148, 150, 151, 153, 155, 158, 159, 161, 162, 164, 165; experiential 4, 5, 22, 60, 150, 163

liability 97, 105

luggage 25, 32, 43, 49, 62, 63, 75 77, 84, 85, 89, 92, 93, 95, 101, 108, 118, 121, 123 126, 142 144, 155, 156; allowance 75, 76; carry-on 62, 63, 76, 77, 123 125

meals 3, 24, 28, 41, 42, 67, 68, 77, 78, 80, 81, 86, 90 93, 95, 111, 118, 127, 129, 135, 137, 138, 144, 149, 154

money 6, 11, 23, 24, 26, 27, 30, 31, 35 37, 39, 42, 47, 48, 58, 73, 75, 76, 86, 87, 89, 91 94, 99, 104, 121, 124, 143

multicultural 10, 163

NAFSA x, 12, 11, 12, 52 54, 113, 162

open-minded; see intercultural, tolerance

parents vii, x, 14, 18, 20, 50, 61, 64, 104, 105, 107, 110, 111, 121, 158, 161

participants 19, 36, 82, 86, 98, 104 106, 108; selection 12, 27, 77, 81

passport 30, 31, 33, 34, 53, 64, 72, 73, 82, 83, 95, 105, 116, 122, 124, 126, 142

pedagogy viii, 2, 5, 22, 163, 164

planning v, vii, viii, xi, 4 7, 10, 13, 14, 16, 17, 19, 21, 23, 26 33, 35 41, 43 49, 51 53, 56, 58, 63, 73 75, 77, 78, 80, 81, 86, 89, 91 93, 97, 98, 100 102, 104, 105, 107, 110, 114, 116 119, 121, 123, 127 129, 134, 137, 140, 141, 153, 155, 158; accommodations 41 42; budget 36 37, 47 49; crisis 52 55; curriculum 26 28; itinerary 22 24, 25 26, 28 29, 34 35, 43 46; timeline 29 33

receipts 48, 49, 80, 111, 118, 120, 125

recruitment 14, 19, 35, 74, 87, 89, 103, 109, 110, 112, 114, 121, 163

registration 19, 83, 98, 99, 101, 103, 107, 110, 112

reimbursement 31, 80, 83, 92

responsibility v, 12, 19, 30, 35, 97 99, 104, 105, 107, 112, 113, 118, 137, 143, 144, 147

responsibility, faculty 148; financial 17, 19, 32, 36, 39, 49, 50, 82, 84, 87, 89, 91, 92, 97 100, 107, 111, 117, 118, 142, 143, 163; institutional support 87, 98, 99; legal 113, 114, 118, 120; time-commitment ix, 13 16, 19, 20, 29, 30

responsibility, students 2, 25, 29, 30 34, 59, 64

responsibility, university 6, 14, 18, 19, 26, 29, 38, 40, 48, 52, 80, 81, 85, 87 90, 92, 94 98, 100 106, 112, 117, 119

169

INDEX

responsible party vii, 14–17, 19, 25, 39, 45, 52, 65, 77, 81, 88, 92, 94, 98, 99, 104, 105, 108, 117, 125, 127, 145, 150, 158

safety 15, 16, 22–25, 39, 44, 54, 79, 84, 106, 113–115, 118, 120, 125, 137, 143, 145, 151, 152, 155, 158
security 15, 22, 25, 39, 54, 63, 69, 78, 100, 106, 118, 126, 143, 158
sickness *see* illness
study abroad viii, 12, 26–31, 40, 50, 56, 58, 59, 61, 70, 71, 73, 81, 82, 85–90, 93, 94, 97–102, 104–109, 111–113, 116, 117, 119, 146–148, 150–153, 155–165; accessibility 37, 128, 129, 147; challenges 2, 6, 7, 12, 13, 18, 27, 40, 41, 44, 53, 56–60, 63, 64, 71, 72, 77, 101, 107, 108, 111, 119, 134, 139, 141, 142, 145, 146, 148, 149, 151, 154, 156, 157; course-based i, x, xi, 3–10, 13, 14, 19–24, 27–30, 31, 33, 34, 36–40, 53, 54, 56–62, 70, 71, 83, 85–90, 94, 97–101, 104–107, 109, 112, 119, 145, 150, 152, 153, 157–160; course-embedded 5, 74; faculty-led 163; philosophy vii–xii, 8–10; short-term 4–8, 10–12, 35, 113, 153, 164

support x, xii, 2, 4, 6, 19, 27, 28, 37, 40, 70, 73, 74, 87–90, 97, 98, 103, 104, 106, 107, 111, 112, 152–154, 156, 157, 162

third-party 21, 37, 38, 40, 41, 54
tour company 38–40, 74
timeline 12, 21, 29–31, 33, 37, 54, 109
transit 44, 62, 79
transportation vii, 3, 9, 19, 24, 30, 38, 40, 41, 43–45, 47, 63, 73, 74, 78, 79, 86, 90–93, 95, 104, 106, 111, 123, 125, 126, 134, 141, 142, 158; bus 43–46, 63, 78–80, 84, 85, 91, 125, 126, 130, 134, 140, 142, 143, 145, 154, 155; cab 18, 125; coach 44, 45, 46, 79, 84, 125, 134
train 34, 43, 44, 63, 78, 79, 91, 125, 129
travel: agent 26, 37, 38, 40, 84, 99, 100, 129; on-ground vii, 3, 30–32, 38–40, 47, 58–60, 73, 81, 98, 102, 106, 110, 111, 121, 122, 144, 158
travel bookings 13, 26, 39, 43, 44, 77, 82, 142

visa 9, 31–34, 52, 53, 64, 72, 82, 83, 86, 90, 95, 104, 105, 107, 122

Wi-Fi 42, 50, 51, 77, 93, 127
worldview 71, 148

Printed in the United States
by Baker & Taylor Publisher Services